Thirteen
Life-changing
Secrets

Thirteen Life-changing Secrets

Mark Finley
Speaker/director
It Is Written Television

REVIEW AND HERALD® PUBLISHING ASSOCIATION
HAGERSTOWN, MD 21740

The author assumes full responsibility for the
accuracy of all facts and quotations as
cited in this book.

Unless otherwise noted, all Bible verses are from
The New King James Version.
Copyright © 1979, 1980, 1982,
Thomas Nelson, Inc., Publishers.

This book was
Edited by Richard W. Coffen
Designed by Helcio Deslandes
Typeset: Novarese 9.5/10.5

PRINTED IN U.S.A.

98 97 96   5 4 3 2

R&H Cataloging Service
Finley, Mark, 1945-
     Thirteen life-changing secrets.

     1. Christian life.   I. Title.
          230.6

ISBN 0-8280-0977-5

Acknowledgments

As a public evangelist I've met tens of thousands of people in some of the world's greatest cities. This book is about them and their search to discover God's will for their lives. It tells their story, asks their questions, and gives God's answers. In fact, it's dedicated to all truth seekers everywhere. To those honest-hearted people who long to know God better. To those who aren't content with the status quo in their lives. To those who sense the need for something more than they have.

I especially want to thank my sister Dale Slongwhite for taking my file folders full of the basic material and shaping the first draft for this book. Her initial writing saved me hours. I deeply appreciate it. Frances Williams, my secretary at It Is Written, worked hours typing the manuscripts. Her ability to read my hieroglyphic handwriting never ceases to amaze me. Also I praise God for a gifted support team dedicated to sharing God's Word with others.

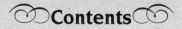

Contents

Before You Turn This Page . . .

For the past 25 years it has been my privilege to conduct public evangelistic meetings in many of the largest cities of the world: Seoul, Korea; London, England; Moscow, Russia; Copenhagen, Denmark; Belgrade, Yugoslavia; Gdansk, Poland; Karachi, Pakistan; and Chicago, Detroit, and Honolulu, in the United States. Although the people in attendance have come from different cultures, speak different languages, have different socioeconomic backgrounds, and enjoy varying intellectual capacities and educational backgrounds, they've been united by one common denominator—they're truth seekers! They seek resolution to the deepest questions of the human heart. They're looking for life-changing secrets.

Thirteen Life-changing Secrets was written for them . . . and for you . . . and for all truth seekers. It tells the story of people who were looking for life-changing answers and found them. It shares the experiences of people who were searching for hope and discovered it. In a straightforward, no-nonsense manner *Thirteen Life-changing Secrets* shares basic Bible truths in a practical, down-to-earth way. I hope that you'll be refreshed as you read it—inspired as you discover new insights from God's Word. But most of all I pray that you'll sense that God longs to reveal His will to you even more than you want to discover it. God isn't playing hide-and-seek with us. He eagerly desires to reveal His life-changing secrets.

After all, Jesus said:

> "Ask, and it will be given to you;
> seek, and you will find;
> knock, and it will be opened to you"

(Matthew 7:7).

As you read these pages, may the deepest needs of your heart be met by a loving Christ who longs to share His will with you. May His answers to your questions meet your heart's desire to know Him. And may the answers you find in His Word give your life a new dimension of happiness.

Mark Finley, It Is Written Television
Thousand Oaks, California

Sold for Six Bottles of Cheap Wine

Teenaged Artyom felt that his future was as bleak as the Siberian countryside where he'd been abandoned by alcoholic parents. Then he learned a life-changing secret—he was on God's mind, because God's concern for us never ends.

The Siberian wind whipped the snow into huge drifts. The biting cold stung Artyom's tear-stained face. With his head down and shoulders slumped, he slowly trudged through the cold night. He knew that within a few minutes he'd be at the train station. At least it would be warm inside. He just couldn't stand it at home any longer. Both his father and mother drank to excess. In some ways his life was like other Russian schoolchildren—biology, math, literature, Russian history—but in other ways, it was remarkably different. He spent a great deal of his time trying to stay out of his parents' way. When they got drunk, which was often, abuse was inevitable.

Artyom didn't know that something was missing. He was only a boy fighting for survival. He couldn't know that even then a God of whom he had no knowledge was watching over him, a Communist child, in Siberia.

When Artyom was 9, his parents separated. The children went with their mother, who frequently left Artyom and his little sister Nadia alone. Their mother couldn't hold down a steady job, and she was regularly drunk. One day, in an intoxicated act of desperation, she tucked identification documents into the pocket of 4-year-old Nadia's coat and abandoned the little girl in a railway station.

Artyom's father and mother continued to argue about who would take the responsibility of raising him. Neither one of them wanted it, but they finally agreed on a price. For six bottles of cheap wine, worth a little more than $6, Artyom's mother gave him to his father and left.

✦

Artyom's situation appeared hopeless. Born into an atheistic, Communistic home of alcoholic parents, he was bartered away for six bottles of wine. Certainly he was doomed from the start. What hope could there be?

There's hope in the God of the Bible, who promises: "I will never leave you nor forsake you" (Hebrews 13:5). No matter what the circumstances, no matter how you feel, no matter what others may have told you, God has *not* forsaken you. He didn't forsake a young boy in eastern Siberia, and neither will He forsake you.

The biblical prophet Isaiah takes it a step further. He reassures us: "Fear not, for I am with you; be not dismayed, for I am your God. I will strengthen you, yes, I will help you, I will uphold you with My righteous right hand" (Isaiah 41:10). The God of the universe—the Creator of all—intimately cares for you. He's with you in the heartaches and sorrows of life. He's there to "uphold you"—to support you against any opponent. You don't need to meet the enemies of life alone. You don't need to face its difficulties by yourself. God is there to lift you up—to serve as a buffer of support. He's there to shield you from life's heavy blows.

✦

In high school Artyom joined the Komsomol, the Communist youth organization. He was asked to spy on the other young people in his high school. He submitted to the Communist Party leaders detailed records of the lives of his peers. By this time he was no longer living at home, because he had no place to stay. After days of searching for housing, he learned that a small church needed someone to keep the coal fire burning and to clean the sanctuary in exchange for free room.

Each week Artyom sat in the back row of this small Christian church. Even though he was steeped in atheism, he listened. Little by little he discovered a Creator whose love knows no limit, whose wisdom is infinite, whose strength is greater than any obstacle, whose promises still apply today, and whose concern for you and me never ends. Artyom couldn't resist such a love. Opening his heart to God's irresistible love, he became a committed Christian.

✦

Life can be difficult. Like Artyom, perhaps your life hasn't been easy. Perhaps you've even asked, "Where's God in all this?" Perhaps you're like the teenage girl who recently shared, "I thought that with all He had to do, maybe God had forgotten about me."

No, God hasn't forgotten about you! Despite all He has to do, you're still on His mind. The Bible writer Jeremiah says of God: "The Lord has appeared of old to me, saying: 'Yes, I have loved you with an everlasting love; therefore with lovingkindness I have drawn you' " (Jeremiah 31:3).

I cherish this image of God's drawing me to Him with everlasting love and lovingkindness. Does this verse conjure up an image in your mind as it does mine? Can you see Him standing before you now, gesturing for you to come to Him? When Satan tempts you to view God as a vindictive judge, just waiting for you to do wrong, remember this verse. In lovingkindness He draws you to Him.

Remember also Moses' experience. "And the Lord passed before him and proclaimed, 'The Lord, the Lord God, merciful and gracious, long-suffering, and abounding in goodness and truth' " (Exodus 34:6). The God who knows all about you loves you most. He knows where you were born. He understands the challenges of your childhood. He's intimately acquainted with the problems of your past. With mercy He considers your weakness.

Isn't it ironic that around the world today hundreds of scientists have pointed complicated and expensive instruments into outer space, hoping against hope to pick up evidence of intelligent life, while at the same time the most intelligent of all lives is speaking to their hearts at this very moment by way of a still small voice?

It's really amazing when you think about it. David tells us in Psalm 33:6, 7: "By the word of the Lord the heavens were made, and all the host of them by the breath of His mouth. He gathers the waters of the sea together as a heap." What awesome power! The God who has made each and every individual creature and creation just by the breath of His mouth and who can stoop down and gather all the waters in all the seas into a heap is the very same God whom Jeremiah reports is drawing us to Himself in lovingkindness.

This revelation is both humbling as well as exciting. The God who is all-powerful, who can roll the seas into a heap, wants a relationship with you. I wonder sometimes why people don't RSVP immediately when they receive such a spectacular invitation. "Will you come?" asks God. And some people actually say no. Perhaps it's because they don't understand who God is and His loving concern for their happiness.

I once met a woman who felt that she'd lost everything in life that was of value to her. But worse than even that

14

was the question she couldn't answer: Why? Why had God let this happen? Why hadn't God intervened? She'd prayed. Where had He been? In confusion and despair she sought a Christian counselor and poured out her story. Where was God? Why hadn't He answered her prayer? She hadn't asked for too much. God could have easily answered.

The Christian counselor leaned forward, considered her client for a moment, then seriously responded, "Why do you think the God of the universe would change the course of history for you?"

I can't answer the why in this case. I don't know God's mind and why He chose to answer the prayer of this woman in a way other than she expected. I can only counsel her to remember the promise of Hebrews 13:5 that God will never leave or forsake her. She must cling to Isaiah 41: 10, which promises God's strength in our difficulties.

But I'd also take issue with her counselor. God can and does change the course of history. In the book of Daniel we read: "He changes the times and the seasons; He removes kings and raises up kings; He gives wisdom to the wise and knowledge to those who have understanding. He reveals deep and secret things; He knows what is in the darkness, and light dwells with Him" (Daniel 2:21, 22).

Jerry McAuley's life vividly illustrates God's transforming power. It's a story of dramatic personal comeback.

When Jerry McAuley sailed across the Atlantic from Ireland to America as a boy, he already had seen the worst side of life. He'd been neglected, starved, and beaten. To survive on the streets, he'd learned the fine art of petty theft.

But in the New York City slums of the mid-1800s he experienced even darker terrors. Jerry grew up in a stinking hovel, drinking rotgut liquor and subsisting on what he could steal from peddlers. He soon joined a gang and became a river rat, one of those who raided cargo ships in the harbor at night. By the age of 19 he'd committed every serious crime except murder, and a judge finally sentenced him to 15 years in Sing Sing prison.

Jerry McAuley showed no signs that he'd ever be anything but a menace to society. The brutality of the streets had penetrated to his bones. He knew nothing of school, church, or family life. The only truth he'd learned was what he could command with his fists.

Life in Sing Sing was more fierce than anything he'd yet known. But it did give him time. And Jerry used the time to learn to read. That's when he discovered the world's most remarkable person—Jesus. He found the Bible fascinating and read it through twice.

For a long time it didn't seem possible that God could forgive him for all he'd done. But finally, after an intense struggle, he yielded to God's grace and accepted the fact that God had forgiven him for Jesus' sake.

The change in Jerry McAuley soon became evident to the entire prison. Another kind of life had begun inside him, producing peace and joy. When he was beaten and spit upon, he took it without fighting back. The only time prisoners could communicate with one another was at the supper hour, and Jerry used that time to share his faith in Christ.

After being released from prison, he went through a time of trial. Dismayed by the hypocrisy of some believers he met, his desire for alcohol returned, and Jerry reverted to his old negative habits. But fortunately a friend talked him into visiting a revival meeting, where he found the love of dedicated Christians, and Jerry made a new commitment to Jesus Christ. As a result, he stayed close to believers and close to the Bible, that remarkable account of Jesus Christ. This time the story of redemption sank in for good. The Messiah who had healed the sick, preached to the poor, and lifted up the oppressed began to live His life through Jerry McAuley.

On the streets of New York City Jerry began to work for people whose stories were as tragic as his own had been. He organized a rescue mission, trusting that resources would be provided. They were, and Jerry's ministry grew throughout the years. The McAuley Water Street Mission became the pioneer outreach to people of the streets, setting an example that many others would follow. Jerry labored faithfully and cheerfully among the homeless until his death in 1879.

✦

What's the value of a life? It depends on whom you ask. For Artyom's parents, it was six bottles of cheap wine. For Jerry McAuley, it was a lifework. For God, it was the sacrifice of Jesus on the cross, the promise that He'd never forsake us, the offer of His strength during times of difficulty, the support against our opponent, the changing of the natural consequences of earth's history, the drawing of humanity to Himself.

What's the value of a life—yours, for instance? You're so valuable that the Creator of the universe eagerly waits to throw His arms around you, run His fingers through your hair, lovingly embrace you, let you cry on His shoulder, and whisper in your ear, "You're Mine. I'll never leave you. Don't worry; in the end it's going to be all right!"

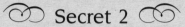

Secret 2
Drug Dealers at the Door

Honolulu was no paradise for Anna because she was addicted to hard drugs. Then she made a marvelous discovery—God's attitude toward us is always one of forgiveness, and His grace can transform our lives.

Anna felt herself caught in the stranglehold of an intense struggle. Her modest apartment was located in the center of Honolulu's drug district. I met Anna while I was conducting a series of lectures on Bible prophecy in that city. She seemed powerless to resist the drug dealers, who brazenly knocked on her door. Daily they urged her to buy another joint. Frequently she gave in! She indulged her growing habit.

At the conclusion of one presentation she pleaded with me for help. "Pastor, I'm so weak! I seem powerless to resist!"

I pointed her to God's promise: "I can do all things through Christ who strengthens me" (Philippians 4:13), and Anna made a marvelous discovery. A new sparkle flashed in her eyes. Jesus really would help her! He'd actually supply His power to deliver her! Two of my associates visited Anna almost daily. The word went out in that drug-infested neighborhood: "Leave Anna alone! She's going straight."

✦

Anna's discovery can make a powerful difference in your life, too! There's power from above for deliverance. God's power is available to you. The Creator's power, which brought the universe into existence, can change your life.

Here's how you can receive it.

Most likely when you fail, you think you're alone. You have the vague idea, the hazy notion, that you're trapped in the prison of your own problems, with no way out. Satan likes to make you think that you're different from everyone else. Your problems are too difficult. Your habits too entangling. Your mountains too high. Your sin too great. You've crossed the line. A line that others haven't crossed.

If you find yourself locked in such a negative, self-defeating thought pattern, let me assure you that this isn't God's voice speaking to you. The Bible paints a very different picture. A picture of a God eager to forgive. A picture of a God longing to set you free from guilt and condemnation.

The apostle Paul declares: "All have sinned and fall short of the glory of God" (Romans 3:23). We've *all* sinned. We've *all* come short of God's glory. We're *all* in need of forgiveness and the Holy Spirit's cleansing power. Christians need a Saviour. We need a Saviour to redeem us from our sins while we're still in sin. If you're waiting to come to God until you're worthy, that day will never come. Satan will see to that!

The Bible says that even in your rebellion God reaches out to you. Speaking of the children of Israel, Nehemiah says: "They refused to obey, and they were not mindful of Your wonders that You did among them. But they hardened their necks, and in their rebellion they appointed a leader to return to their bondage. But You are God, ready to pardon, gracious and merciful, slow to anger, abundant in kindness, and did not forsake them" (Nehemiah 9:17).

God led the children of Israel out of Egyptian bondage. He fed them with manna from heaven six days a week. He

19

directed their path with a pillar of fire by night and a cloud by day. And what was their response? They constructed a golden calf and worshiped it! Unbelievable ungratefulness, wouldn't you say?

How would you react to such an insult? Would you have lashed out angrily at those who despised your best efforts to help them? At the very least you'd probably have turned away from them. But that's not how the Bible tells us God reacted to the children of Israel. Even as they were rebelling, Nehemiah records, God waited to pardon them. He's gracious and merciful, slow to anger, and of great kindness.

While they were sinning, He *didn't forsake them*. Let the impact of this amazing truth sink in for a moment. If your image of God is of a being who deserts you when you need Him most, that image didn't come from the Bible. It's a tragic distortion of God's character. The Bible portrays a God who will stand by you even in your weakness, failures, and rebellion. Nehemiah says that God continues to guide and to demonstrate kindness and to show mercy *even while you're sinning*. That's the important part. You don't need to do something first. The first move is God's. He takes the initiative.

The next move is yours. God allows you the freedom of choice, and He continues to love you no matter what those choices are. There is, however, a move essential on your part in order to receive forgiveness. That move is simply to ask for it, to admit you've done something wrong, and to ask to be forgiven.

"If we confess our sins, He is faithful and just to forgive us our sins and to cleanse us from all unrighteousness" (1 John 1:9). Forgiveness isn't something earned by overcoming sins; it's something received by confessing them. Forgiveness is God's attitude of loving mercy to those who've wronged Him. Forgiveness is part of God's very nature. Your confession of your sins doesn't earn God's forgiveness, but it does enable you to receive it.

True, it might be hard to confess, to admit you've done

something wrong. But when you weigh that against what you receive in return—your heavenly Father's forgiveness—the difficulty pales. Confession. Forgiveness. Guilt dissolved. Cleansing begins.

I like the metaphor Isaiah used to describe God's method of forgiveness. He said: "I have blotted out, like a thick cloud, your transgressions, and like a cloud, your sins. Return to Me, for I have redeemed you" (Isaiah 44:22).

Clouds are a powerful barrier. Sometimes they obliterate the sun's rays. And guilt can obliterate your picture of God. It destroys His image. But it's unnecessary to feel weighed down by guilt. God has blotted out your sins like a thick cloud. He's blotted out your transgressions forever.

The second part of the verse is just as encouraging. It is *after* He has blotted out your sins that He asks you to return to Him. Permit me to reiterate: Returning to Him is *not* a prerequisite to pardon.

The verse brings to my mind an image of a loving father calling out to one of his children. The child has done something she shouldn't have done. She's scared. She's somewhere out in the darkness hiding. The father is looking for her and calling out, "It's OK. I've forgiven you. Don't stay away because of what you've done. Come on home. I still love you."

This is a God I can trust. This is a God I can approach. This is a God with whom I'd like to spend eternity.

God stands ready to pardon. He forgives unconditionally when you confess. He blots out your sins like a cloud, but He also takes it one step further. He forgets what you've done. To Him it's as though you haven't sinned at all. Hebrews 8:12 says: "I will be merciful to their unrighteousness, and their sins and their lawless deeds I will remember no more."

Amazing! An omnipotent and omniscient God can actually forget. Of all the things He can do perfectly, I'm thankful that the one thing He can't do is remember what I've done wrong after I've confessed it to Him. That's more than you or I will do for ourselves at times! Forgive and forget. You've noticed that sometimes your mind won't let you rest. You play again and again the instant replays of your sins, worrying and wondering how God could ever forgive you, or ever love you, or redeem you. But He can. Let Him do His job. Your job is to request forgiveness, believe that He's granted it, and relax in His arms. Forgiveness is rooted in God's very character.

David states: "Blessed is he whose transgression is forgiven, whose sin is covered" (Psalm 32:1). The Hebrew word translated "blessed" means happy, very happy. A forgiven person is a happy person. A great weight has been lifted from the shoulders. One has a clean slate. An opportunity to start again. And how good that feels!

After you've accepted God's forgiveness for your sins, the Bible says that you must then extend that forgiveness to those who've wronged you. "And be kind to one another, tenderhearted, forgiving one another, just as God in Christ also forgave you" (Ephesians 4:32).

Carrying around a mental list of who's wronged you can be a real burden. The apostle Paul asks you—no, he commands you—to be tenderhearted to others, forgiving others. The apostle urges you to stop keeping score with those who've offended you. Attitudes of bitterness and revenge are destructive. Isn't it more enjoyable to be planning a tender act toward someone than plotting revenge?

The apostle gave this counsel years before scientists knew how closely connected mental and physical health actually are. God commands you to be forgiving not only for the benefit of the one who has wronged you, but for your own benefit as well. Harboring negative feelings, clinging to traumatic experiences, refusing to grow beyond the hurts, can sometimes cause physical problems that are worse than the original barb sent our way. Ulcers, heart attacks, and poor emotional health can, at times, be induced by lack of forgiveness. Forgiveness, on the other hand, encourages the healing process to begin.

◆

Not long ago I received a letter from Maria, who attended a series of my presentations in the Midwest on Jesus' loving forgiveness. She said that after attending my lecture on forgiveness, she'd finally found the strength to forgive her father.

From the ages of 2 through 5 Maria was the victim of incest. She recalled that all during her childhood she was "a lover in the woods, by the seashore, in the garden." Her father, an alcoholic, attempted to strangle her when she was 5 because he feared that she'd tell someone what he'd done to her. Throughout her childhood Maria felt alone and terribly empty inside. She started to neglect herself. She didn't eat, and she cried frequently. Her parents blamed her for her destructive behavior.

As an adult Maria felt unworthy, guilty, dirty, and lost, and she often contemplated suicide. She woke up one morning paralyzed in her neck and back. She tried physiotherapy and various forms of gymnastics, but grew worse and worse.

Only when she understood God's forgiving, outgoing, unconditional love did healing begin. Although she realized that she was in no way responsible for her father's horrible actions, she did sense that she too was a sinner who also needed forgiveness before a holy God. Now she could forgive her father. For the first time in many years she felt clean, forgiven, cleansed. "I now really have peace of mind," she wrote. "Thank you for letting Jesus speak to me through you." Forgiveness is therapeutic. It's a powerful healing agent.

◆

Maria also sought counseling as part of her healing. For many people, developing a relationship with a Christian counselor is a necessary part of working through hurt and pain. The guidance and compassion of one who not only understands your pain but also can point you in the direction of the great Comforter can be a valuable asset in your Christian walk.

It isn't difficult to forgive someone who's wronged you and admits the error, is it? But what about the person who's turned his or her back? Who has aimed a few blows in your direction and then walked away, maybe even laughing? Is it possible to forgive such individuals as well?

If you're to follow Jesus' example, certainly! Just as the first move when you sin against God is His forgiveness, so the first move when someone sins against you is your forgiveness to the offender. Remember, Ephesians 4:32 says that you're to forgive others in the same manner God has forgiven you. He stands ready to forgive before you even ask. He's your example. To forgive before you hear the words "I'm sorry" may seem impossible. And it is, on your own. The only way you can forgive someone who's wronged you and doesn't deserve your forgiveness is to realize that Christ has forgiven you yourself when you didn't deserve it. The only way you can release someone from your condemnation is to realize that Christ has released you from His condemnation. The only way to be a forgiving person is to sense that you're first forgiven.

Of course, it isn't necessary to stay in an abusive relationship to prove that you've forgiven. Maria's forgiveness of her father didn't require her to live in her father's home or to allow him to continue his abuse of her. What it did require was an attitude of kindness, tenderheartedness, and forgiveness.

Forgiveness—of the sins you've committed against God and of the sins others have committed against you. Forgiveness! Won't you allow it to begin a transformation in your life today?

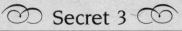

When Life Isn't Fair

After 25 years of marriage, Tom left Carol for a younger woman. Resentment shattered Carol's fragile existence until she learned a life-changing secret: It's better to rest in God's arms than to grant anger a resting place in the pit of one's stomach. God gives us courage to cope when we forgive others as He's forgiven us.

L ife isn't fair. It's as simple as that. You read about Maria in the previous chapter, about the sexual abuse she endured at her father's hands. That shouldn't have happened. But it did, and Maria's life was altered as a result. That wasn't fair.

Here's one thing you can be certain of. When life isn't fair, God still is. He has not only the ability to rebuild lives, but also the all-consuming desire to get started right away!

Tom was seeing another woman, and Carol didn't want to believe it. It was too difficult for her to accept. Her emotions screamed against the prospect of a divorce. After 25 years of what she thought had been a happy marriage, Tom was now leaving her for a woman 25 years younger.

When Carol discovered her husband's affair, she was emotionally devastated. Their youngest son planned to be married within the year. She'd been looking forward to the time she and her husband would spend at home, alone once again. She saw it as a time to renew their first love. And now she asked the unanswerable Why? Why had Tom chosen to leave her after she'd given so much, after she'd lived her life for him? Gradually her questions turned to bitterness, then to anger. It wasn't fair. It just wasn't fair!

After the divorce Carol was overcome with loneliness and deep depression. The more she thought about what had happened, the more incensed she became. One night, in deep distress, she cried out to God for strength to cope with this unbearable situation.

Soon she started sorting things out in her mind. Her husband had ruined her past, but she wouldn't allow him to ruin her future. In spite of what he'd done, in spite of her bitterness, she could *choose* to forgive him.

Carol recalled Ephesians 4:32: "And be kind to one another, tenderhearted, forgiving one another, just as God in Christ also forgave you." And she made a choice to let the words of this text seep into her soul, transform her heart, make her a new woman.

If Christ could forgive *her* sins when she had been His enemy, she could forgive Tom even though he'd become *her* enemy. If Jesus could reach out to her when she didn't deserve it, she could reach out to Tom when he didn't deserve it. She could ask Jesus to give her a new attitude and a transformed spirit. Through Him she could become tenderhearted, kind, and forgiving.

As their son's wedding day approached, Carol experienced peace at the prospect of facing Tom and his new wife. They prearranged a meeting in the church on Saturday evening at 6:00, shortly before the wedding practice. Carol arrived early to sit alone in the quietness, meditating and praying that God would help her have the grace to forgive Tom. She asked Him to take away her bitterness and resentment.

Shortly she heard the creak of the large oak church door. She heard the familiar footsteps echo throughout the sanctuary. Quietly she rose and turned to face Tom. Clutching his arm was an attractive, smartly dressed young woman.

Carol walked up to Tom and put her hand on his shoulder. "Although I was deeply hurt by what you did," she said,

"I want you to know that I've forgiven you." Addressing the young woman, she said, "Although it's going to be tough, I'll do everything I can to make this weekend pleasant for you." She turned, and the three of them walked down the aisle and sat together in the front pew, waiting for the wedding practice to begin.

✦

What gave Carol the ability to forgive like that? How is it possible to overcome the bitterness, the anger, the resentment that can so often occur when life isn't fair? The Bible provides principles that can really make a difference.

Do you have deep hurts that move you to anger? In order to move beyond your anger, you must first admit that you're angry. Have you tried to suppress the emotions simmering just below the surface? Are you basically keeping them in check at the not quite boiling point? By not allowing them to be seen by others, you may try to fool yourself into believing you have everything under control. "I'm not mad," you hiss through gritted teeth. And somehow you think that's the Christian way of dealing with negative emotions.

Be honest with yourself. Be honest with God. Admit you're angry and having a difficult time coping with the predicament. Hebrews 4:13 says: "And there is no creature hidden from His sight, but all things are naked and open to the eyes of Him to whom we must give account."

God already knows what's going on inside, so there's no use trying to hide it from Him. And there's great benefit in sharing it with Him. Offer a prayer something like this: "God, I'm angry. I acknowledge the fact that my emotions are out of control. I don't know what to do about it. Please help me."

By being honest, by admitting the problem and your helplessness to solve it, you unleash God's power within you. You give Him permission to begin His work of restoration. A work that you're incapable of doing yourself, but a work that must be accomplished if you're to continue growing closer to Christ.

It's important to identify the cause of your displeasure. God asked Cain: "Why are you angry?" (Genesis 4:6). In other words: "Cain, why are you so angry? What's the cause of your fiery emotions?" It's possible to have pent-up emotions and not know exactly why. It's possible to be overwhelmed by feelings. At times it's necessary to step back and ask What's really going on here? Why do I feel the way I do? Is my anger justifiable?

Why was Carol angry? Because her husband left her? To deal honestly with her feelings, Carol needed to probe deeper than the obvious. She might have been angry because she felt abandoned or lonely. It was difficult to accept the fact that her financial plight would cause her standard of living to plummet. She had to alter dramatically her daily routine. Carol needed concrete answers to the question Why am I angry? in order to begin dealing with her pain.

It's possible for emotions, rather than conscious decisions, to control the life. Ecclesiastes 7:9 says: "Do not hasten in your spirit to be angry, for anger rests in the bosom of fools." "Rests in the bosom of fools"—now there's a phrase to ponder! In addition to bearing the pain, who wants to sink to the classification of a fool?

It's one thing to become indignant with your injustices, but it's quite another thing to permit that angry turmoil to rest in your bosom. To overtake your emotions. To assume control of your actions. Anger, unchecked, can drive you to do things you'd never choose to do in another state of mind. It can grow like a cancer within you. It can overshadow whatever good things may be compensating for the evil.

So you're angry. What do you do now? How do you deal with it? Give your rage to God. David says: "Rest in the Lord, and wait patiently for Him; do not fret because of him who prospers in his way, because of the man who brings wicked schemes to pass. Cease from anger, and forsake wrath; do not fret—it only causes harm" (Psalm 37:7, 8).

Wouldn't you rather rest in the Lord's arms than grant anger a resting place in the pit of your stomach? Don't fret over the person who causes wicked devices to pass, the Bible counsels us. Cease from anger; forsake wrath. And most important, trust the Lord to take care of you and the circumstance that you find intolerable. Allow Him to dissolve your anger. Allow Him to comfort you. Allow Him to work it out.

How many times have you prayed the Lord's Prayer? You can probably recite it from memory. But I wonder if in all the rote recitation you've forgotten the meaning packed within its few short paragraphs. In response to the request of one of His disciples—"Lord, teach us to pray"—Jesus Himself prayed what we call the Lord's Prayer as a model to follow. The Master prayed: "And forgive us our sins, for we also forgive everyone who is indebted to us. And do not lead us into temptation, but deliver us from the evil one" (Luke 11:4).

Forgiveness is an important step in dealing with anger, which causes bitterness, which causes resentment, which stifles spiritual growth. The previous chapter addressed at length the importance of forgiveness. Since God has forgiven you for what you've done to Him, you can be confident that He'll give you the gift of forgiveness for what others have done to you. True heartfelt forgiveness of those who've wronged you is a gift you can request from God.

So deal with wrath quickly. Don't let it accumulate and multiply within your heart. Don't let it rest in your bosom. If possible, address the anger the day it occurs, and then let a new day dawn with a positive focus. Ephesians 4:26 advises: "'Be angry, and do not sin': do not let the sun go down on your wrath."

What a wonderful way to handle life's irritations! To

identify the source of the nettles and to address the problem the same day before the sun goes down. Sometimes problems multiply needlessly when allowed to fester. Taking a proactive approach as Scripture suggests, before your temper explodes, is a healthy approach to dispelling ire.

✦

Joseph had every reason to be angry. He'd done nothing wrong, yet 10 of his 11 brothers despised him. They were jealous that their father had expressed his love to their younger brother by playing favorites. They were further enraged when he told them of several dreams that put them in a position of subservience to him. He dreamed that their sheaves of grain bowed to his, that 11 stars were obedient to him. And because they were envious, they plotted to kill him.

One of the brothers, Reuben, persuaded them to sell Joseph to a band of itinerant merchants. Their lie to their father, Jacob, that Joseph had been killed by wild animals broke his heart. Joseph's bloody coat seemed to prove their tragic story—Joseph was dead!

Meanwhile, Joseph was sold as a slave to Potiphar, captain of the guard in Pharaoh's palace. And God watched over Joseph in a plight that should have caused the young boy much grief. Instead of wallowing in his misfortune, the 17-year-old stayed true to his childhood faith. He trusted God. The Bible says: "The Lord was with him; and whatever he did, the Lord made it prosper" (Genesis 39:23).

Potiphar's attractive wife attempted to seduce Joseph. True to his conscience, he fled. Might this have been the world's first false sexual harassment case? Potiphar's wife lied. Joseph was unjustly tossed into prison. Had he compromised his integrity, Joseph could have easily thought, *I've been unjustly condemned by my brothers and sold into slavery, and now I'm unjustly imprisoned and perhaps will be executed un-*

justly. Life just isn't fair!

After two years in prison Joseph won Pharaoh's favor by interpreting his dream of an upcoming famine. Pharaoh made Joseph second in command, and for the next seven years he gathered food throughout the land of Egypt. The Bible says that he "gathered very much grain, as the sand of the sea, until he stopped counting, for it was without number" (Genesis 41:49).

When the famine struck, the Egyptians cried out to Pharaoh for help. Pharaoh directed them to Joseph, who opened up the storehouses and sold them what he'd collected. The famine was widespread. Eventually Jacob sent 10 of his sons to Egypt to buy food.

Remember, these are the same 10 men who had sold Joseph into slavery. Who had the upper hand now? Joseph, of course! He could have refused to sell food to those who had plotted to kill him, those who had sold him into slavery for 20 pieces of silver. He had every reason to be infuriated. Had he retaliated, we might have labeled it righteous indignation.

But Joseph had given his resentment to God. He'd allowed God to control his life, allowed Him to turn a potentially disastrous set of circumstances into something more spectacular than anyone could have imagined. Joseph, rather than getting even, fell upon the necks of his brothers and kissed them. He filled their sacks with food. He insisted they move their families near him for the remaining five years of the famine.

He said to them: "But now, do not therefore be grieved nor angry with yourselves because you sold me here; for God sent me before you to preserve life" (Genesis 45:5). Can you imagine it? He who had every right to be furious with the brothers who'd tried to ruin his life admonished *them* not to be angry! What a testimony to the power God can supply when we grant Him access to our inner heart! What a model for those who believe they have the right to harbor rage against someone who's ruined their life!

✦

It's true. Life isn't fair. Since we live in a world dominated by sin, bad things do happen to good people. We do at times get what we don't deserve. Our lives are fragile. We live continually on the edge of disaster. But despite it all, despite what happens to us, despite the pain we endure, there's one thing we can be assured of. When life isn't fair, God still is. He's there in the heartache and tragedy. Life may let us down; our friends may let us down; our own family may let us down; but God never does. His love is constant. His kindness is never-ending. In spite of what happens to us, He does something within us. He gives us the courage to cope. He dissolves our doubts. The divine Comforter gives us comfort. The Peacemaker gives us peace. The Light of the world illuminates our darkness. The Pearl of great price gives us new treasures of life.

✦

Listen to these words of Joseph to his nervous brothers: "But as for you, you meant evil against me; but God meant it for good" (Genesis 50:20). And for each of His children, God is able to bring something good out of something intended only for evil.

Let go of anger. Give it to God, then step aside, and see what He'll do next.

Secret 4
Death in the Crib

Tragedy struck the Jarod family while teenager Jenny baby-sat for them. Their infant suffocated in his crib. One life-changing secret helped the Jarods cope with their unfathomable grief—Jesus is coming again to call a halt to our planet's tragedies and will wipe away every tear.

The dew sparkled like diamonds. The warmth of the sun's rays felt invigorating on my customary morning walk through the picturesque Georgia hills. My wife, Teenie, and I were living in Wildwood at the time, where I spent most days as a youth pastor, teaching and sharing the Bible with college-age young people. As often as I could, I began the day with a hike on the quiet mountain trails around our home. The strength I gained from these early-morning walks gave me renewed courage to face the challenges of the day . . . and this day I would surely need it.

The phone was ringing when I returned home. "Pastor Finley?" a trembling voice asked.

I confirmed she had the right number.

"I'm the nurse at Dr. Adams' office in Trenton. Do you know a teenager by the name of Jenny?"

"Yes. I've studied the Bible with her on a number of occasions. Is something wrong?"

"I'm afraid so, Pastor," she answered. "Jenny was baby-sitting for the Jarod family. The baby's parents were not home. The baby suffocated in the crib, and Jenny just walked into our office with the dead baby in her arms.

She dropped him on the floor and ran out screaming for us to contact you to help her." The nurse paused. "Pastor, can you drive to Trenton immediately? Can you find Jenny and give her some comfort? And Pastor, can you . . . can you tell the baby's parents that he's dead?"

I jumped into my car and sped around the windy curves on the narrow country roads between Wildwood and the county seat, 12 miles away. Thoughts swirled inside my head. Should I contact Jenny or the baby's parents first? Since I didn't know where Jenny might be, I decided to head for the home of the baby's parents.

As I pulled into the driveway, I noticed two little boys playing with toy cars and trucks in the dirt to the right of the porch. The younger one looked up and said with little expression, "Mister, the baby's dead." So obviously the parents knew by now as well.

I entered the home and found the mother huddled on the couch beside her husband. He had a comforting arm around her shoulders, but she was crying uncontrollably. Her sobs wrenched my heart. I couldn't imagine what it would be like to go through this horror.

I walked over to where the young mother sat and put my hand on her shoulder. Through her tears and sobs she looked up and said, "Pastor, thank you for coming."

For a few moments I said nothing at all. And then simply, "Ma'am, I can't possibly understand your pain. I can't possibly understand the heartache and the sorrow you're going through. I've not lost one of my children. But there *is* One who can understand. His Son died—not a crib death like your child—but He willingly left the glory of heaven to die on the cross so that death for us would not be forever.

"The grave could not hold Him. He burst the bonds of that tomb. He was resurrected from the dead, and He lives. Because Christ lives today, your boy can live again too.

"Jesus understands your heartache. He knows your sorrow. There's a day coming when the living, all-powerful Christ will descend the corridors of the sky, and life will be new again. The righteous dead will be resurrected, and the righteous living will be caught up to meet Him in the air."

I opened my Bible and read words of hope to the grieving couple—the only hope to which we can turn when facing the ultimate dilemma of death: the hope of Jesus' second coming.

✦

One of the most beautiful and well-known passages of the Bible is found in John 14:1-3: "Let not your heart be troubled; you believe in God, believe also in Me. In My Father's house are many mansions; if it were not so, I would have told you. I go to prepare a place for you. And if I go and prepare a place for you, I will come again and receive you to Myself; that where I am, there you may be also."

Thousands of people, perhaps millions, have taken solace in these words since Jesus spoke them nearly 2,000 years ago. The Son of God has assured us that upon His return to heaven He'd begin arranging for our arrival as well. He longs to have us with Him. The desire of His heart is to spend eternity with us. He declares before the heavenly universe that through His death on the cross our sins are forgiven. The power of His love has redeemed us. He has given us a new heart—we now have new natures, new desires, and a new power to live the Christian life. Before cherubim, seraphim, and all the angelic host He declares that we're safe to save.

On many occasions Jesus promised the disciples that He'd come again. And as He was ascending to heaven, two angels appeared to remind them of that pledge. You can imagine how the disciples must have felt after the events of the previous week, never mind the past three and a half years. They'd left their livelihoods to follow Him. They'd traveled all across the countryside as they listened to and learned from Him. They'd witnessed His capture and murder. Afraid, they'd huddled in the upper room. He'd miraculously appeared and delivered them from their fears. And now He was leaving them again?

He knew their insecurities and didn't wish to leave them comfortless, so He sent two angels with a message. We read about it in the first chapter of Acts. "Now when He had spoken these things, while they watched, He was taken up, and a cloud received Him out of their sight. And while they looked steadfastly toward heaven as He went up, behold, two men stood by them in white apparel, who also said, 'Men of Galilee, why do you stand gazing up into heaven? This same Jesus, who was taken up from you into heaven, will so come in like manner as you saw Him go into heaven' " (Acts 1:9-11).

Someone has estimated that the Bible records more than 1,500 prophecies of Jesus' second coming. For every prophecy of His first advent mentioned in the Old Testament, there are eight texts predicting His second coming. Once in every 25 verses in the New Testament the return of our Lord is mentioned. Jesus has made every effort to alert us that He's returning to take us home. He hasn't tried to keep it a secret, and neither will He come in secret on that day.

"Behold, He is coming with clouds, and every eye will see Him" (Revelation 1:7). His return isn't going to be some sort of clandestine meeting in the wilderness that only a few will know about. The Bible says that *every* eye shall see Him. You'll look up into the sky one day, and you'll see a very small cloud coming closer and closer, getting bigger and bigger. And upon that cloud will sit the Son of man, the Redeemer come to take His children home.

His return will be like lightning flashing across the sky. "For as the lightning comes from the east and flashes to the west, so also will the coming of the Son of Man be" (Matthew 24:27). Don't worry; you won't miss this event!

36

The whole sky will be lit up. Everyone around the globe will view Jesus' second coming. No matter where you happen to be at the moment, you'll feel compelled along with everyone else to look up and see the glory of it all.

In addition to seeing it, you'll hear it. "For the Lord Himself will descend from heaven with a shout, with the voice of an archangel, and with the trumpet of God. And the dead in Christ will rise first. Then we who are alive and remain shall be caught up together with them in the clouds to meet the Lord in the air. And thus we shall always be with the Lord" (1 Thessalonians 4:16, 17).

Can you imagine the Lord Himself calling you to come home? Can you imagine God's trumpet blast of victory? Now, that will be something to hear! Don't worry about missing it. It will clearly be an audible event. I wonder what God will actually say when He calls you and me from His heavenly throne? Perhaps He'll say something like this: "Children, it's time to come home. You've suffered enough. There's been enough pain, enough heartache, enough sorrow. There have been enough shattered homes and broken lives. There have been enough war-torn nations and bombed cities. There's been enough drunkenness, drugs, and death." Whatever it is, I'll be listening—I can tell you that!

The Bible informs us that the incident will be so compelling that the righteous dead will be wakened and will rise up to meet Him. I can imagine that their voices will add to the praise as they meet Him in the air. Can you envision how many of them there will be? Everyone who has followed the Lord since the beginning of earth's history—all together rising in the air! What a scene! What a hope! It's certainly worth living for. It will be a glorious day!

Matthew's Gospel adds: "For the Son of Man will come in the glory of His Father with His angels, and then He will reward each according to his works" (Matthew 16:27). The angels are coming with Him! They've been watching the battle between good and evil since Lucifer challenged

God's right to rule. Certainly they'll be included when the dual is finally settled.

The righteous, obviously, will be delighted to see Him. I love the way Isaiah describes their reaction: "And it will be said in that day: 'Behold, this is our God; we have waited for Him, and He will save us. This is the Lord; we have waited for Him; we will be glad and rejoice in His salvation'" (Isaiah 25:9). It will be a time of celebration for those who love the Lord! They've waited for Him, and now He's come.

The day, however, will hold different emotions for the unrighteous. They'll cry to the mountains and rocks: "Fall on us and hide us from the face of Him who sits on the throne and from the wrath of the Lamb! For the great day of His wrath has come, and who is able to stand?" (Revelation 6:16, 17).

It's a tragic scene, isn't it? Revelation 6:15 tells us that the ones who are now crying out for the mountains and rocks to hide them were powerful individuals. Their brilliant minds, their corporate positions, their huge bank accounts, cannot save them now. Turning their backs on God, they've lived self-centered lives. They've looked for answers in all the wrong places: money, materialism, parties, sex, cheap thrills, drugs, alcohol—anywhere but God. They've chosen another way of life. The Christ who redeems the righteous must destroy sin, or it will corrupt the universe again. Christ's glorious presence, which warmly welcomes His children, consumes the wicked.

He's returned this time as the King of kings, leading His armies of heaven. He returns at last as triumphant Lord. "And He has on His robe and on His thigh a name written: KING OF KINGS AND LORD OF LORDS" (Revelation 19:16).

Why so many biblical prophecies foretelling Jesus' second coming? Why draw attention to this event again and again and again? I think the last book of the Bible holds the answer. "And the Spirit and the bride say, 'Come!' And let him who hears say, 'Come!' And let him who thirsts come. And whoever desires, let him take the water of life freely" (Revelation 22:17).

Jesus doesn't want us to come to this event unprepared. He desires that all should be saved and brought home to live eternally with Him in heaven. His second coming heralds the beginning of a new world in which "affliction will not rise up a second time" (Nahum 1:9). He wants all His children to choose to be there.

Sin will be stamped out forever. Death will be no more. Babies will be restored to the arms of their mothers. "And God will wipe away every tear from their eyes; there shall be no more death, nor sorrow, nor crying; and there shall be no more pain, for the former things have passed away" (Revelation 21:4).

There *is* hope for a hopeless world. There *is* comfort for parents who have lost children, for all Christians who have lost loved ones. There *is* relief from the tragedies of this world—from sorrow, pain, and suffering. That hope is found in the soon return of our Master, the second coming of Jesus.

∽ Secret 5 ∽
Huck Finn's Prayers

After Miss Watson showed Huckleberry Finn how to pray, he decided that "there ain't nothing in it." Yet despite the profound silence that followed and which perplexed Huck—and us—prayer is a life-changing secret. It helps us delight in God's friendship while we wait for Him to work more powerfully.

Miss Watson she took me in the closet and prayed, but nothing come of it. She told me to pray every day, and whatever I asked for I would get it. But it warn't so. I tried it. Once I got a fish-line, but no hooks. It warn't any good to me without hooks. I tried for the hooks three or four times, but somehow I couldn't make it work. By-and-by, one day, I asked Miss Watson to try for me, but she said I was a fool. She never told me why, and I couldn't make it out no way.

"I set down, one time, back in the woods, and had a long think about it. I says to myself, if a body can get anything they pray for, why don't Deacon Winn get back the money he lost on pork? Why can't the widow get back her silver snuff-box that was stole? Why can't Miss Watson fat up? No, says I to myself, there ain't nothing in it" (Mark Twain, *The Adventures of Huckleberry Finn*, p. 17).

✦

Have you ever felt like Huck Finn, who made these comments on prayer? You've prayed for a sick relative . . .

and she died. You've prayed for health . . . and become ill. You've prayed for guidance . . . and heard only silence. You've prayed for your kids . . . and they've rebelled. You've prayed to get out of debt . . . and sunk in deeper.

If everyone who has gone through these experiences would shout "Amen" the sound would echo around the world!

Does this mean there's nothing to prayer? That it's only a phenomenon in which the people praying fool themselves into believing someone has heard?

Let's candidly discuss prayer. What is it? How can we pray more effectively? Does intercessory prayer really achieve anything? One thing is for certain—the Bible is full of assurance that God longs to answer our prayers. "Thus says the Lord who made it, the Lord who formed it to establish it (the Lord is His name): 'Call to Me, and I will answer you, and show you great and mighty things, which you do not know' " (Jeremiah 33:2, 3).

The purpose of prayer is to communicate with an all-powerful, personal God. Prayer is first and foremost communication. It's fellowship with the God who made us. Prayer isn't some kind of magic formula to get God to do what we want. In the communion of prayer there's an atmosphere of peace resting in His love, enjoying His presence, and experiencing the sheer delight of His friendship.

Jeremiah assures you and me in this text that the Creator of the universe wants to, is eager to, communicate with us. He desires to impart His wisdom on you. He invites you to enter into a relationship with Him so that He can make Himself known to you. This text invites you to call upon Him, and when you do He promises to answer, to show you "great and mighty things." Not just ordinary things. In this passage God promises to reveal great and mighty things.

The purpose of prayer is to lead the person praying into oneness with God's mind, to enable the petitioner to have a deep fellowship with Him. Revelation 3:20 says: "Behold, I stand at the door, and knock: if any man hear my voice, and open the door, I will come in to him, and will sup with him, and he with me" (KJV).

Where does a great deal of family communication take place these days? It's around the supper table, when family members finally have a moment to sit down and share the adventures of the day. (At least it used to be that way.) Cheers for the accomplishments, affirmations in failure, encouragement in the trials. Shared laughter, debated ideas, hope for the future. Sooner or later it all comes out around the supper table.

That's why I like the word "sup" in this text. God desires to converse with you on all aspects of your life—everyday things, the pain, the jubilation, the questions. He's like any other member of the family around the supper table, with one major difference. God is never like an abusive parent who puts His children down. The heavenly family isn't a dysfunctional unit. Although we at times may feel worse after an argument around the supper table, we come from the presence of God in the process of being healed, refreshed, and invigorated with the calm assurance that He has our best interest in mind.

One of the purposes of prayer is to praise God. Don't you think it's a time to open up and trust Him with the things of your heart that you might not want to share with anyone else? "While I live I will praise the Lord; I will sing praises to my God while I have my being. Do not put your trust in princes, nor in a son of man, in whom there is no help" (Psalm 146:2, 3). Prayer is a time to sing praises to God. The Psalms can be a wonderful help in this because they're replete with praise. Repeat them. Meditate upon them. Marvel at how glorious the Lord is!

Another purpose of prayer is to offer thanks to God for the important role He plays in your life. "In everything give thanks; for this is the will of God in Christ Jesus for you" (1 Thessalonians 5:18). It's sometimes helpful to make a short list of specific things you're thankful for before you pray. Then kneel down and speak the thanksgiving of your heart back to God aloud.

God loves to hear your praise. His heart thrills when you thank Him. Thanksgiving brings health to your entire being as well. At the same time, He never gets tired when you express your concerns. Your difficulties never weary Him. The apostle Peter, whose life was filled with trial and who often came to Jesus with his weaknesses, instructs: "[Cast] all your care upon Him, for He cares for you" (1 Peter 5:7). Life can be difficult. Life is often a battlefield. You've undoubtedly felt battered at times. And those problems—some petty, some great—can add up to a very weighty burden if you don't unload it. That's why Peter invites you to cast the full weight of your anxiety onto the Lord. Why? Because He cares for you.

Consider the power of intercessory prayer—praying for others. The apostle Paul says: "For this reason we also, since the day we heard it, do not cease to pray for you, and to ask that you may be filled with the knowledge of His will in all wisdom and spiritual understanding" (Colossians 1:9). Do you understand the significance of this text? Paul is saying that he constantly prayed for the Colossians, asking God that they be filled with the fullness of the Word of God. Throughout Paul's writings, in Galatians, Ephesians, Philippians, Colossians, he constantly says, "We're praying for you; we're praying for you; we're praying for you."

Intercessory prayer has always been part of the Christian community, but now the medical community is giving it attention as well. A review of medical literature has revealed 130 studies that were conducted during a 20-year period. One study, for example, had been conducted at San Francisco General Hospital by Dr. Robert Byrd. It was a double-blind study. Neither the medical personnel nor the patients knew about the prayers. Because the mind can release positive chemical endorphins that enable the body to heal itself, Dr. Byrd wanted to be sure this wasn't a factor in his study.

He chose 393 patients who had coronary bypass surgery and wrote out details regarding half those patients. He then distributed these notes to Christians in the San Francisco area, asking them to pray for these specific patients. The results were indisputable. The prayed-for group, which you remember had no knowledge of the prayers, recovered more quickly than the unprayed-for group. They had fewer complications and needed less medication.

All this research leads to the conclusion that from a purely scientific point of view, something happens when we pray that doesn't happen if we don't pray.

I am aware that many dedicated Christians may have legitimate concerns and even questions about some aspects of such research. Nevertheless, even though it can be difficult to reproduce the results of some experiments, the medical literature seems to provide some evidence that prayer does make a difference.

But why pray for someone else? Isn't God doing everything He can to save your son or your daughter before you pray? Isn't God doing everything He can to reach out to your loved ones even before you ask? If so, why pray?

In the controversy between good and evil, in the powerful conflict between Christ and Satan, although Christ is doing everything He can before His people pray, He can do so much more if they do pray. Christians don't pray because God is doing nothing. They pray because they desire to see God work more powerfully. Prayer opens the channels of God's blessing.

First John 5:16 says: "If anyone sees his brother sinning a sin which does not lead to death, he will ask, and He will give him life for those who commit sin not leading to death. There is sin leading to death. I do not say that he should pray about that." In other words, if someone hasn't committed the unpardonable sin (the sin unto death) and you pray for that person, God will hear that prayer and work miracles. Prayer becomes the conduit of God's grace. Human beings can become the link on the earthward side that opens up God's blessing.

Prayer serves many purposes. Through prayer you can communicate with your Father in heaven and develop a friend-to-friend relationship with Him. Through prayer you can praise Him and thank Him for what He has done for you. Through prayer you can cast your burdens upon Him and walk away comforted, knowing that He cares and can be trusted to watch over you no matter what. Through prayer you can make requests on behalf of others. Prayer is a powerful tool that God urges each of His children to employ.

✦

Probably one of the most unusual experiences of my life occurred in Thousand Oaks, California, when I witnessed the results of 47 years of prayer. In 1946 Paul and Ruth Boynton began a term of mission service in Tehran at the Iran Training School. One of the students there was 16-year-old Ludmila, a Russian girl. She listened as the new principal, Pastor Boynton, spoke of Jesus Christ, and she memorized the English words to the hymn "I Come to the Garden Alone." She studied Bible lessons, but before she could make a decision for baptism, her parents decided to return to Russia.

With tears in his eyes Pastor Boynton encouraged Ludmila to continue her studies. "If the doors ever open in Russia," he said, "and if Seventh-day Adventists ever come to preach God's Word, please, Ludmila, do attend. I'll be praying for you."

And he kept that promise—for 47 years. Often Pastor Boynton remembered the 16-year-old with the flair for languages and the beautiful soprano voice. Where was she in that vast country with its 11 time zones? Had the message of Jesus blossomed in her heart, or had it been extinguished by the cold realities of atheistic Communism? For 47 years he prayed for Ludmila by name.

Decades passed, and in 1993 I traveled to Moscow to preach in the Olympic Stadium. The iron curtain had come down at last! At the time of my meetings, I'd never heard of Paul Boynton or Ludmila Titova. Then one evening a well-dressed Russian woman in her early 60s approached me at the conclusion of one of my lectures. She spoke in beautiful English and asked if I knew Paul Boynton. "He taught me from the Bible in Tehran 47 years ago," she said. "He told me to attend Seventh-day Adventist meetings if they should ever come to Russia, so that's why I'm here this evening."

I was thrilled that she had attended the meetings after having been introduced to Jesus 47 years previous, but I had to admit to her that I didn't know Paul Boynton. We spoke for several minutes, and then she wrote down her name and address for me. I looked forward to visiting with her on subsequent evenings, but an illness prevented her from coming to the last meetings. Our team left Moscow without hearing from her again.

Several months went by, and then one weekend I was in Orlando, Florida, with a group of It Is Written supporters. Right before the meeting one of our staff members asked, "Would it be all right if my former Bible teacher had the morning prayer?"

"Of course," I said, and listened as Paul Boynton was introduced! I could hardly wait for the meeting to end, and I immediately confronted him. "I know something about you," I told him.

"What's that?" he asked.

"That you were a missionary in Iran."

"That's true," he confirmed.

"You taught at the language school."

"Yes."

"And you had a student named Ludmila."

Well, I thought he was going to reach out and pick me up off the ground! "Ludmila!" he cried. "What can you tell me about her?"

I shared how we'd met in Moscow. Tears came to his eyes as he realized that God had looked after the precious student for whom he'd prayed for many decades. I realized then that we had to pursue this unusual story, but alas, I had misplaced the scrap of paper on which Ludmila had scribbled her address.

I returned to Moscow the next month, but was unable to locate Ludmila. My associate, Royce Williams, was scheduled to return to Moscow a month after that, and he made that slip of paper a matter of prayer.

"God," he prayed, "help Mark find Ludmila's address."

Two days before Royce was scheduled to fly out, I located her address. It was crumpled in the back of a drawer. Had she moved during the months since we'd been in Moscow? Had the illness that prevented her from attending our last meetings been terminal? We had no way of knowing until Royce flew to Moscow and did a little investigating. He wrote several messages and tucked them under the apartment door at the address Ludmila had handed to me months before. After several days Ludmila's son telephoned to say that his mother was in Los Angeles visiting relatives—just a few miles from the It Is Written facility!

We arranged for a reunion between Ludmila and Paul Boynton at the Thousand Oaks Seventh-day Adventist Church. I don't believe there was a dry eye in that congregation when Ludmila Titova stood to sing "I Come to the Garden Alone." Before her solo, however, she told of the little Russian New Testament given to her by a relative before leaving Iran, how it passed the border check unnoticed, and how she'd carefully hidden it for so many years. And then this 63-year-old woman sang the gospel song she'd learned as a 16-year-old girl in Tehran.

✦

I'm glad that Paul Boynton's understanding of prayer was not the same as Huck Finn's! For 47 years Pastor Boynton had prayed, believing all the time that God would work it out.

Answers to prayer don't always occur in the time frame we think they should. Answers to prayer don't always occur in the manner we think they should. But answers to prayer do occur. Sometimes it might even take 47 years.

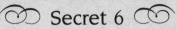

Escape From Hell's Kitchen

If you'd known Jim Finley back in the 1930s, you'd have predicted that his rootless life in Hell's Kitchen and later in Harlem—27 different apartments and 15 different schools—had doomed him. But Jim found a life-changing secret: God promises guidance, and His power is greater than flawed heredity and stronger than an impoverished environment.

J im was just another New York City slum kid, like thousands of others growing up in a section of the city aptly labeled Hell's Kitchen. He had a shaky home life, no money, no future, and certainly no security. Survival necessitated learning life on the street. And Jim learned those lessons well.

Social psychologists debate which affects our actions more—heredity or environment. They argue which is a greater determinant of who we'll become—that mix of chromosomes by which we're genetically configured, or the day-to-day events that surround us. In light of the powerful influence of heredity and environment, some specialists would call Jim a born loser. He never knew his real father, and his environment consisted of the worst ghettos of New York. But one factor made all the difference—a factor that most psychologists won't acknowledge.

Jim, my dad, came to New York City at the age of 9. He traveled alone on a train from Chattanooga, Tennessee. From his birth he'd been shuttled from aunt to uncle to cousin, whoever would take him for a while. He had the distinct impression he was only a burden. But now his mother had sent for him. She'd recently married a tugboat captain twice her age. Maybe this time it would work. Possibly now she'd be able to squeeze him into her life. Perhaps this time she could give him the stability he desperately needed.

I suppose my grandmother, Beulah, meant well when she reached out for my father on that New York City railroad platform back in 1933. But he drew back from this woman who'd become a stranger. Confused and tired, he dodged her and ran into the crowd. She finally captured him and brought him home to Hell's Kitchen—a slum whose hopelessness hung heavy in the air. The lives of the poverty-stricken families, hungry children, and rabble-rousing teenagers all played out their dramas for all to hear through the thin walls between the tenement apartments. They were evident on the graffiti-covered walls and noisy, crowded streets below.

This was the world in which my father had to learn to survive. When a group of bullies pinned him to a wall and taunted, "Speak, Southern boy. Let's hear you speak," he realized the kind of skills he'd need in order to survive on the streets. With each syllable he whispered, they laughed and slugged him in the stomach and smashed him in the face. You couldn't be different here. You had to blend in. Be one of the guys. Dad learned that the law of the street was the law of the fists. The strongest survived. The weak often didn't. With little emotional help from home, he learned to fend for himself.

Although my grandmother was hopeful that life would finally level out for the family, it never did. Her husband drifted from job to job. He'd work sometimes as a tugboat captain, sometimes as a custodian of cheap apartment houses. Part of that job included throwing onto the street the homeless who dozed in the hallways.

The family was constantly on the move, constantly scrounging for life's necessities. My dad had to get used to standing in line for free cans of beans and stew and wearing the khaki pants that announced to the world he was on welfare. He remembers that the only coat they could afford for him one winter was missing a sleeve—burned away in a store fire. So the coat was given to a poor kid for free.

I remember as a young boy lying on the living room floor with my dad one rainy Saturday afternoon and asking, "How many places do you remember living in, Dad?"

He laughed and began to count. He could remember 27 apartments before he turned 17 and 15 different schools before he dropped out in the eleventh grade.

With this erratic school record and unstable home life, my father had a hard time keeping up with the other students. And to make his personal agony worse, he knew something was missing. He looked around the many classrooms in which he was the new kid, and noted other students who were progressing enthusiastically. *They're gonna succeed*, he thought. *Someday they're gonna be somebody. Someday they'll have respectable jobs and nice places to live, and their kids will have all the things I never had.* He knew he was being robbed of something valuable. Something elusive, hazy. Something he could glimpse only from a distance.

On Friday nights the Salvation Army in Hell's Kitchen picked up boys like him so that they could give them a meal and take them to a preaching session. Dad tolerated the sermon as part of the bargain. After a while he even took up the French horn, though his mother tried to discourage him. She lied to him by telling him he had only one lung. But Dad persisted, and eventually played in a Salvation Army band.

One Friday night Dad was playing with the band in Times Square when the leader of the group asked for band members to give testimonies. Dad looked around at the people who'd paused to listen to the music, and before he could figure out why, he hopped onto a soapbox and began to speak. "It's not easy for a guy like me to get up here," he said, "'cause I ain't no better than the rest of you. I've been goin' to the preaching sessions at the Salvation Army for a few months now, and I ain't always been listening, but some of it's been sinking in. And I just gotta say that I think there's something to this religion bit, and someday I'm gonna find out what it is." He was only a young teenager with poor role models in his life, engulfed by a world that should have dragged him down. But somewhere in the muddle of it all, he heard God's voice and listened.

When he went home that night, he found a note on the door. "We moved to Harlem. Here's the address." Hell's Kitchen was like the Promised Land compared to Harlem! Harlem's poverty, its degradation, its gangs, its crime, were simply overwhelming. Dad's life was a subway to disaster. He was on a train with a one-way ticket of broken dreams, shattered hopes, and utter despair.

With each new neighborhood, each new drab apartment, each new starting again, my father felt the entrapment of his environment closing in on him. The downcast faces surrounding him all shouted the same frightening message: "There's no hope. No way to escape. You're trapped here."

But the people at the Salvation Army preached a different message. They said it was possible to have a new life. They said the Bible was filled with bright promises. A battle waged in Dad's mind between what was and what could be. The streets required him to be tough. And he was. But still, maybe someday, he thought, he'd find another way.

By the time my dad was 17 he knew his mother still viewed him as a burden. So he ran away from home. First he hid out in the attic of his friend Skip, who sneaked up leftovers from the family's meals. Later he crossed the river to Jersey City, where he lived with his stepbrother and took care of an elderly blind man living in the home. Finally he tried what seemed to be the ultimate escape—the Navy. In the discipline of military service he found a measure of stability. He also found freedom from the restraints of home. He stayed out late, caroused from bar to bar, and stole a few cars. He felt relief that no badgering parents were around.

This is the man who raised me in a Christian environment! I owe my first steps in Christ to him. I owe my ministry to him. Just watching how he shares his faith with others has taught me more than all the schools of evangelism I've attended. It's been my privilege to travel around the world, sharing the good news of Christ. But in all my preaching I've never gone far from the inspiration I received at my father's side. Jim Finley is, in my opinion, a wonderful man of God. My three sisters and I have always cherished his gentleness as a father, his integrity as a businessperson, and his dedication as an active layperson in his church.

So how did he get from there to here? How did he get out of Hell's Kitchen? The answer to that question is very important, because it's a path that you too can choose. No matter what personal hell you're involved in, no matter what circumstance life has dealt you, there's a God who is reaching out to you.

As for my father? In short, he didn't get out of Hell's Kitchen. Hell's Kitchen got out of him. From a very young age Dad sensed the inner tug of the Holy Spirit upon his heart. Although his ugly environment strongly pulled him toward evil, he felt God working in his life, drawing him to right and truth.

His Navy career brought him to the submarine base in Groton, Connecticut, where he met a wonderful woman named Gloria. Before they married two years later at the age of 20, my dad shared the longing of his heart with his sweetheart. "There's something I want you to know," he said. "I believe there's a religion out there that teaches the truth, and someday I'm going to find it. When I do, I'm going to join it." In the quiet support we've all come to appreciate throughout the years, Mom affirmed his determination.

After his discharge from the Navy, Dad went to work in a machine shop in Westerly, Rhode Island. He was the boss on the night shift. Daily he met with the leader of the day shift to exchange production reports. One day he noticed a Bible on the foreman's desk. "I've been wanting to learn more," he said. "More about the Bible and God and what it all means."

The man offered to study the Bible with Dad. This was the beginning of the journey of Dad's life. It would bring him further from his New York City upbringing than his travels in the Navy ever could. Dad was a hungry Bible student. He prayed and diligently studied God's Word. Immediately he realized that this was what he'd been searching for his whole life. The principles of the eternal kingdom stood out strong and clear.

At age 33 he made a commitment, a commitment to the God who'd gently and persistently wooed him since his boyhood. And Dad never looked back. The God of Scripture performed a great transformation in my father's life.

◆

It's a truth most psychologists have difficulty acknowledging. There's a power in the universe greater than the pull of heredity or environment—the power of the living God. The apostle Paul gives this wonderful assurance: "If anyone is in Christ, [that person] is a new creation; old things have passed away; behold, all things have become new" (2 Corinthians 5:17).

Now, I'm not going to turn this into a fairy tale and tell you that all Dad's problems were solved. He had more than his share. More than he'd want me to reveal to you. But the difference is that he didn't go through those times of trouble alone. He had complete confidence in God to guide him. He knew Someone who cared.

Throughout his life as a boy he'd longed for guidance. His youthful heart had yearned for someone who really cared to give him the advice he so much needed. Once he'd personally accepted Jesus Christ, he discovered the source of personal guidance that he knew was there but didn't know how to find.

The apostle James counsels: "If any of you lack wisdom, let [that person] ask of God, that giveth to all . . . liberally, and upbraideth not; and it shall be given" (James 1:5, KJV). I love this Bible promise! Maybe it's the phrase "giveth to all . . . liberally" that means so much to me. Do you realize how powerful this statement is? God hasn't chosen just a few people to whom He'll impart His wisdom. "To all," He says. To each and every one who asks. Did you notice that He promises a *liberal* dose of wisdom? Not just a sprinkling of wisdom, but a generous portion!

You might not be familiar with the word "upbraideth." Webster gives this definition: "to criticize severely; to scold vehemently." The inclusion of this particular word heightens the meaning of the text. Have you ever gone to someone for advice and had it given to you scornfully? Or the tone of voice implied "Don't ask me again"? That isn't God's way. He distributes His wisdom generously, without reproach. He's happy to share it with anyone who asks.

Do you lack wisdom? Has your life become so complicated that you can't see through the fog? Do you want to get back on track? Then ask God for His wisdom. Spend time praying. Attempt to discover what He wants you to do. Ask Him for His solutions to your problems. Don't expect a voice shouting the answer from heaven. No, God won't write the message in the sky. But if you sincerely seek Him, you'll have a settled confidence of what He wants you to do. In time He'll gradually reveal His will.

Why is it that prayers are sometimes not answered? The psalmist explains it this way: "If I regard iniquity in my heart, the Lord will not hear" (Psalm 66:18). That's a pretty direct declaration. There's no need to ponder its meaning or look up any words in the dictionary. Those who cherish sin, who say "Take anything but this, Lord," may hinder God from answering their prayers.

Analyzing motives is also important when asking for God's guidance in daily decisions. "You ask and do not receive," says James, "because you ask amiss, that you may spend it on your pleasures" (James 4:3). For instance, if the petitions you bring to the Lord in prayer would enhance your selfishness, He may not grant them. Personally, I'd have it no other way! I'd rather go without a selfish desire for a few short years on this earth than to risk losing eternity over it.

Remember, the Lord hasn't left you alone to ponder your alternatives and worry about the consequences. Many times your choices will involve a biblical principle. The Bible is a rich source of guidance; often God will direct you as you read His Word. "Your word is a lamp to my feet and a light to my path" (Psalm 119:105).

When the way seems dark, allow the Scriptures to illuminate your path. The life experiences the biblical writers chose to record weren't randomly selected. They were divinely inspired to be used as instruction for the generations of believers who followed.

God also wants you to seek instruction from wise Christian counselors who have demonstrated their trust in Him. In Proverbs 11:14 we read: "Where there is no counsel, the people fall; but in the multitude of counselors there is safety." Is there someone you know whose Christian witness exudes godliness? A pastor, a parent, a friend, a church member? With all the information you gather to make a decision, consider what these ambassadors of God also have to offer. They may have learned something in their lives that may be of substantial benefit to you.

Look for providences—divinely ordained circumstances that indicate which way you should go. These providences are like signposts that help in the process of decision-making. They don't take the place of God's Word, sound judgment, or good common sense, but they can assist you. "My son, give me your heart, and let your eyes observe my ways" (Proverbs 23:26).

After you've earnestly prayed about a decision, consulted God's Word, thought carefully about it, sought counsel from Christians you trust, and watched for providential leading, make the wisest decision possible, believing that God Himself is leading you.

One of my favorite Bible texts on guidance is found in the book of Isaiah: "The Lord will guide you continually, and satisfy your soul in drought, and strengthen your bones; you shall be like a watered garden, and like a spring of water, whose waters do not fail" (Isaiah 58:11). I like the imagery of this text—an irrigated garden, a spring that never runs dry, fat bones. This is how the Lord will continually guide those who sincerely seek Him.

✦

Peter Marshall, one of America's well-known ministers of a previous generation, allowed God's voice to guide him throughout his life, beginning as a young teen growing up in Scotland. One summer night he decided to take a short-cut across the moors on his way home. The area was noted for limestone quarries, but he was familiar with the terrain and felt he could safely navigate his way.

Though the night was starless and inky black, he set out through the rock and heather. He could sometimes hear the far-off bleating of sheep and the wind rustling through. Occasionally a moor fowl he disturbed fluttered up noisily. Otherwise he was very much alone in the night.

Suddenly he heard a voice call out with great urgency: "Peter!"

Halting, he called back into the dark, "Yes, who is it? What do you want?"

No response. Just a bit of wind over the deserted moorland. He concluded he'd been mistaken and walked on a few more steps. "Peter!" he heard again, this time with an even greater urgency. "Peter!"

He stopped in his tracks, squinting into the blackness of the night. Who was there? He leaned forward, stumbled, and fell to his knees. Reaching out a hand to the ground before him, Peter felt nothing but thin air. A quarry! Sure enough, as Peter carefully felt around in a semicircle, he discovered that he was on the brink of a limestone pit. One more step and he would have plummeted to his death. One more step—if he hadn't heeded God's voice.

Out there in the desolate moor Someone knew him, and Someone cared. That same Lord is interested in your life as well. He's not some far-off being who set the world spinning and stepped aside, His business finished. Rather, He's a God who has promised through inspired biblical writers to provide wisdom when we lack it, to instruct and teach us in the way we should go, to light a lamp before our path.

Peter Marshall heard God calling him and lived. My father, Jim Finley, heard God calling him and experienced a life-changing transformation. If it was possible for these two men of that generation, it's also possible for you.

Do you need guidance in your life right now? Are you at a crossroad? Are you facing some critical decision? Do you need someone to lean on? However much you long for His guidance, He longs to give it to you even more!

Parts of this chapter were adapted from Sandra Finley Doran's *Nobody's Boy* (Review and Herald Publishing Association) and are used by permission of the author.

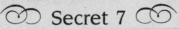

Talking to the Dead Can Be Dangerous

When at midnight the Filipino army officer awakened to howling wind and banging shutters, his eyes gradually focused on the form of his beautiful wife hovering above his bed. But she was dead! A single life-changing secret kept him from embracing this apparition—the biblical insight of what death is really like.

The night I preached about death at a series of meetings in the Philippines a typhoon ripped through the island. One of the individuals who attended that meeting was a Filipino army officer who listened attentively to what the Bible teaches about death.

That night he was awakened about midnight by the roaring of the wind. The shutters of his house flapped wildly against the clapboard. The wind howled through cracks around his window. The rain pounded noisily against the panes. And as this Filipino officer opened his eyes, he saw a beautiful form above his bed. He was astonished. It appeared to be his wife!

Her skin was an unblemished olive color. Her hair was long, flowing, and black. Her magnificent brown eyes looked clear and appealing. He was convinced it was his wife, but not as she'd been at age 60. This was his wife returned as she was at 35.

She reached out to him and said in a voice he couldn't mistake, "Darling, I've missed you. I long to embrace you."

Even as he longed to reach out and hold her, he remembered the lecture earlier in the evening. He remembered what the Bible says about death. "As the cloud disappears and vanishes away, so he who goes down to the grave does not come up. He shall never return to his house, nor shall his place know him anymore" (Job 7:9, 10). He recollected a verse from Revelation that says: "For they are spirits of demons, performing signs" (Revelation 16:14). He recalled 2 Corinthians 11:14: "Satan himself transforms himself into an angel of light."

And he knew that no matter how much this being looked like his wife, no matter how much she sounded like her, this form above his bed was *not* his wife. So he looked up and said, "In the name of Jesus Christ, be gone. Be gone, in Jesus' name!"

And when that Filipino military officer told me the story the next day, he said, "Right before my eyes that form disappeared."

✦

All across the world today men and women have a renewed fascination with the subject of life after death. Near-death experiences are common. Out-of-the-body experiences are accepted by millions. Books on near-death experiences have been runaway best-sellers.

A few years ago only a few individuals on the edge of science were interested in the topic. Today dozens of physicians, psychologists, biologists, and anthropologists are doing near-death experience research. There's actually a *Journal of Near-Death Studies* and an International Association for Near-Death Studies. Pollsters now estimate that some 8 million Americans have had near-death experiences. One book, *Life After Life*, has sold 7 million copies. Another, *Embraced by the Light*, stayed on the New York *Times* best-seller list for weeks.

What are we to make of all this? Just what *does* happen to people who seem to take incredible journeys at the moment of near death? Are these just hallucinations? Are they the beginning of an actual journey toward heaven and God? Or is there something occult, even demonic, involved in this shadowy otherworld of floating spirits?

I'm certainly no expert on what happens to human beings physiologically at the moment of near death. But I believe that all of us can make a few commonsense judgments on the basis of the overall evidence.

First, we need to remember one thing about all the people who relate near-death experiences—none of them really died. As physicians tell us, a person isn't dead when the heart stops or when breathing ceases; a person is dead when so many brain cells have died that there's no possibility of revival.

Second, many near-death experiences resemble hallucinations. The mind can play extraordinary tricks on us—especially at times of great trauma. The brain can take us on vivid journeys. And it can take us to places that are real and places that are *not* real.

Third—and here's the most important piece of evidence—the Bible doesn't teach that human beings have an immortal soul that leaves the body at the time of death. In fact, Scripture very clearly states that we receive immortality only after the second coming of Jesus Christ.

The apostle Paul described that event. "For the Lord Himself will descend from heaven with a shout. . . . And the dead in Christ will rise first" (1 Thessalonians 4:16). He also plainly told the Corinthians that at Christ's second coming "this corruptible must put on incorruption, and this mortal must put on immortality" (1 Corinthians 15:53).

The Bible—Old Testament and New—pictures death as a sleep with no conscious thought, a sleep that only Christ's coming awakens. In fact, Scripture refers to death as a sleep no less than 50 times. And although the Bible refers to the human soul many hundreds of times, it never once says it's immortal.

Jesus compared death to sleep. He said to His disciples: " 'Our friend Lazarus sleeps, but I go that I may wake him up.' Then His disciples said, 'Lord, if he sleeps he will get well.' However, Jesus spoke of his death, but they thought that He was speaking about taking rest in sleep. Then Jesus said to them plainly, 'Lazarus is dead' " (John 11:11-14).

There's no doubt in this text or in the story that follows regarding the status of Jesus' friend Lazarus at the time. He was dead. There can be no confusion here. The funeral was over. His body had been embalmed with the typical Jewish spices, wrapped in the traditional burial cloth, and placed in a cavelike tomb.

Several days had passed before Jesus arrived. He stood before the tomb and called Lazarus to "come forth!" (verse 42). (Note that Jesus didn't say, "Lazarus, come down.") Martha said to Him: "Lord, by this time there is a stench, for he has been dead four days" (verse 39). Where was Lazarus these four days? Certainly not in heaven. The record is absolutely silent on any trip to glory. If Lazarus had gone to heaven, he would have had quite a story to tell about the glory of eternity. How could he have held back from sharing his experience? And wouldn't he have complained about returning to live once more on this sin-plagued planet after having been to Paradise? Lazarus had nothing to report about his four days in the grave. He went on to live years after this event, and the Bible doesn't record his ever revealing any details of those four days.

Why not? Because, as Jesus stated to His disciples, Lazarus was just sleeping. The Bible says: "The living know that they will die; but the dead know nothing" (Ecclesiastes 9:5). David referred to death as a sleep: "Lest I sleep the sleep of death" (Psalm 13:3). The book of Job compares death to a sleep: "So man lies down and does not rise. Till the heavens are no more, they will not awake nor be roused from their sleep" (Job 14:12).

When God created Adam in the Garden of Eden, He breathed into him the breath of life. The book of Genesis records it this way: "And the Lord God formed man of the dust of the ground, and breathed into his nostrils the breath of life; and man became a living soul" (Genesis 2: 7, KJV). The verse does not say that God put an immortal soul into Adam. It says that he *became* a living soul. The inference is clear: the soul is not a separate entity from the person. So, based on that text, this formula can be written: Dust + Spirit = Living Soul. A living soul in the Bible is the same thing as a living creature or person.

When human beings were first created, God formed the body from the dust of the ground, breathed into Adam the breath of life, and the first human being became a living soul. What happens at the time of death? Death is creation in reverse. Ecclesiastes 12:7 says: "Then the dust will return to the earth as it was, and the spirit will return to God who gave it." The body returns to the dust, and the spirit returns to God. Note that the text says the spirit returns to God. It does not say that a soul returns to God.

And here's where people make a mistake. They don't understand what the Bible means when it uses the word "spirit." Is it something conscious—does it think? Job 27: 3 describes the spirit in these terms: "All the while my breath is in me, and the spirit of God is in my nostrils" (KJV). Thus, spirit = breath. In other words, the spirit is the same as God's breath of life, or His life-giving power. At Creation God breathed into Adam the breath of life, and at the time of death that spark of life returns to God.

Ponder with me just a moment the implications of believing that a person soars directly to heaven at the time of death rather than resting in the grave until the Second Coming. Could that person really enjoy the time there? What if she looked down to see her son captured and tortured during a war? What if he could see his daughter abused by a stepfather? What if he or she observed from this celestial position the writhing pain of a loved one dying from AIDS? Would that really be heaven—or more like a living hell?

You see, God's way is the best way. It's the merciful way. When you die, you'll just rest until all the heartache and suffering of the earth is over. Psalm 115:17 couldn't be any plainer: "The dead do not praise the Lord, nor any who go down into silence."

The Bible uses the words "soul" and "spirit" hundreds of times, but never once does it use the phrase "immortal soul" or "immortal spirit." Don't you think that if the soul were immortal, the Bible would put the words "immortal" and "soul" together at least once in all those references?

First Timothy 6:16 says that only God has immortality. We receive immortality when Jesus comes again. It is at the Second Coming that the righteous dead will be raised to life. "For the Lord Himself will descend from heaven with a shout, with the voice of an archangel, and with the trumpet of God. And the dead in Christ will rise first" (1 Thessalonians 4:16). Until then they're asleep, unconscious of the passage of time, as secure as if they were in the arms of Christ Himself until the resurrection. Would the Bible say that the righteous dead rise at the Second Coming if they were already in heaven? Certainly God wouldn't expect them to reenter the tomb, would He?

✦

Why is it important to understand this biblical truth? Because, as in everything else, Satan wishes to deceive us. When he tempted Eve to take the fruit of a particular tree in the Garden of Eden, he said to her: "You will not surely die" (Genesis 3:4). His words contradicted what God had said about the forbidden fruit. He cautioned that "in the day that you eat of it you shall surely die" (Genesis 2:17).

And today Satan seeks to perpetuate his version. He claims that humans have immortality. That when they die they continue to live in some other form. And that's only part one of his deception. Part two is that you can contact your dead relatives. Now, if you understand what the Bible says about death—that it's only a sleep and that the "dead know not anything"—you'll realize that it's preposterous to think you could communicate with them. But if you thought they were living on somewhere, the devil could lure you into believing that you could speak with them again.

And so Satan has set in motion a scenario that he'll play to its full extent at the time of the end. To those who believe they can consult with their deceased loved ones, he'll send apparitions with supposed messages "from the other side." It wouldn't surprise me if he even tried to impersonate the Second Coming. He'll teach truths contrary to the Bible. He'll try any number of deceptions by impersonating the form and voice of a loved one.

Back in the mid-sixties an Episcopal bishop from New York City by the name of James Pike thought he could communicate with the dead. He wasn't able to reconcile himself to the suicide of his son Jimmy, and thought the dead boy might try to contact him. Bishop Pike believed that the Bible contained good moral principles, but rejected its teaching authority. He thought Christ was a good man but not the Son of God, and he didn't believe the Bible instruction about what happens at death.

Bishop Pike moved to England to spend time at Oxford and Cambridge universities, where he studied biblical manuscripts. One day upon returning to his room, he noticed a number of bizarre occurrences. Cards containing Jimmy's picture, which he'd placed on the nightstand, were opened. The clocks in the room had stopped at 8:20—precisely the time that his son had committed suicide. Safety pins he'd left closed on his dresser were opened at odd angles. The mirror was tilted at an angle. Jimmy's clothes had been taken from a box and strewn around the room.

Bishop Pike felt that Jimmy was trying to contact him, so he visited one of London's spiritists. The medium brought up the form of the bishop's son with this message: "Yes, Father, I am in heaven, an eternal place, but don't talk to me about a Saviour. Jesus was a good man, but not the Saviour. . . . This is a wonderful place of joy and love. Jesus was a wonderful, enlightened spiritual teacher. He's here with the other cosmic masters."

After a series of these visits, Bishop Pike was instructed to go to Jerusalem to meet his son in the Judean desert. He should have known that he should not reject the teaching of the Bible, but he chose to ignore that and went with his wife to the desert, where they wandered in the Judean hills, searching for Jimmy. The bishop became dehydrated, and his wife ran for help, but it was too late. Bishop Pike died in the desert, looking for his dead son. He should have known. The biblical counsel on death was clear, but he ignored it.

It may seem comforting to some to believe that a deceased relative is now safe in heaven. That he or she is living in one of those mansions Jesus promised to prepare. That he or she is reunited with relatives who have gone before and is now enjoying immortality with them. But after we've opened the Bible and analyzed the evidence on this topic, it's clear that Jesus' way is much better.

The Bible says that in the last days "false christs and false prophets will rise and show signs and wonders to deceive, if possible, even the elect" (Mark 13:22). However, you need not be deceived.

The day will come when you'll be reunited with loved ones in heaven. Jesus will keep all those promises He has made about the heavenly kingdom He's preparing. "And behold, I am coming quickly, and My reward is with Me, to give to every one according to his work" (Revelation 22:12). There's light at the end of the tunnel. Not some hazy, ethereal figure, but the glorious presence of the resurrected Christ. He *will* come again.

The second coming of Christ is real. Heaven is real. Since Jesus has conquered the grave, you needn't fear death. Death is but a brief sleep until the Lord's return. It's a brief pause before the Second Coming. What confidence! What hope! What assurance! What good news! Since Christ lives, you too can live again. The grave could not hold Him, and it will not hold you.

You can see your loved ones again. In His hands your life and theirs are secure. Don't you want this kind of assurance in your life? Don't you want to look forward to this face-to-face reunion with Christ and your loved ones?

God wants you to have a very clear picture of what awaits His children on the other side of the grave. He hasn't left you to guess. With Him your future life is secure.

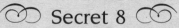

Mysteries of the Mummies

More than 140 scientific papers written during the past 40 years reveal that the members of one Christian denomination know eight simple steps to healthful living that enable them to live four to nine years longer than the rest of the population. You, too, can benefit from these life-changing secrets!

Dr. Rosalie David of Manchester University in England has an unusual job. She's part of a medical team that does autopsies on Egyptian mummies. She's unwrapped many interesting clues regarding the lifestyle of that ancient civilization. Those of us living in the twentieth century and racing toward the year 2000 can learn a great deal from her studies. The ancient pharaoh Ramses II is one of the mummies that researchers have examined. A massive heart attack killed him. His arteries were clogged with fat. Another researcher, Dr. Rufois, X-rayed hundreds of mummies. He discovered that they suffered from arthritis, heart disease, rheumatism, syphilis, cancer, obesity, and tooth decay.

Who could have imagined that the health problems plaguing society today existed thousands of years ago? Who would have thought that a civilization much closer to God's creative hand would have deteriorated so rapidly? What caused the diseases of the Egyptians? Why did they die of these particular maladies? Archaeologists have learned much about the lifestyle of the ancient Egyptians. They've learned that some Egyptians consumed an excessive amount of alcohol, were overweight, and ate a lot of sugary foods. Many had a diet extremely high in fat content. And immorality was rampant.

As God was leading the Israelites out of Egyptian bondage, He promised them: "If you diligently heed the voice of the Lord your God and do what is right in His sight, give ear to His commandments and keep all His statutes, I will put none of the diseases on you which I have brought on the Egyptians. For I am the Lord who heals you" (Exodus 15:26).

The Egyptians, of course, didn't live by the health principles outlined by God. As a result, they suffered lifestyle-related diseases. God promised the Israelites that if they followed His statutes, they wouldn't endure the same infirmities.

✦

Some people think that death and life, disease and health, is a spin of the wheel of fortune. If the pointer stops at you, illness and death are inevitable. For many of our modern-day illnesses, however, this is just not true. If people would take responsibility for their actions, they'd have a greater measure of health.

It's true that not all disease is caused by the actions of the sufferer. The disciples asked Jesus who had sinned, "this man or his parents?" when referring to a man blind since birth. "Jesus answered, 'Neither this man nor his parents sinned' " (John 9:3). Unfortunately, sickness, disease, and tragedy are manifest in a world afflicted by sin.

On the other hand, we do live in a world of cause and effect. Many diseases can be prevented. People can feel better physically, emotionally, and spiritually by taking care of themselves.

Third John 2 says: "Beloved, I pray that you may prosper in all things and be in health, just as your soul prospers." God wants you to be healthy. He wants you to enjoy life to the fullest. When Jesus came to this earth, He said: "The thief does not come except to steal, and to kill, and to destroy. I have come that they may have life, and that they may have it *more abundantly*" (John 10:10).

More than 140 scientific papers have been written in the past 40 years about the amazing longevity of members of the Seventh-day Adventist Church. In fact, Adventists are among the most highly studied population in the world. Astoundingly, Adventist males have a life expectancy ranging from 4.2 to 9.5 years longer than their non-Adventist counterparts and Adventist women have a life expectancy that is 1.9 to 4.6 years longer. Another scientific study showed that if a 35-year-old man began following the lifestyle that will be outlined in this chapter, he has a good chance of adding 12 years to his life expectancy!

Clearly, health principles aren't meant to restrict human freedom. They aren't some legalistic requirement that must be followed in order to gain God's pleasure. Rather, violation of them results in natural consequences.

Americans spend a lot of time these days discussing the cost of health care and a new health-care plan for all Americans. But did you know that there's an ancient health-care plan that God designed thousands of years ago? Statistics indicate that if you follow this plan, you can add years to your life.

Would you like to live longer and healthier? Would you like to avoid the suffering so many have inflicted upon themselves? Would you like a new start? NEWSTART is an acronym and coined and trademarked by a lifestyle center in northern California called Weimar. It summarizes the essential principles of a healthy lifestyle to eight basic principles. Here they are:

Nutrition. When God created the human race, He provided the best possible diet. "I have given you every herb that yields seed which is on the face of all the earth, and every tree whose fruit yields seed; to you it shall be for food" (Genesis 1:29). To the first man and woman God gave a diet of fruits, nuts, grains, and vegetables. A magnificent vegetarian diet. Today nutritionists advocate a diet low in fat and high in carbohydrate. The best example of this is a vegetarian diet—the diet given to us by our Maker. The people in Bible times who followed God's plan lived long and abundantly healthy lives.

Not until after the Flood, when all plant life had been destroyed, did God give the human race permission to eat meat. Later He specified what meat His people should eat: "And you may eat every animal . . . having the hoof split into two parts, and that chews the cud. . . . These you may eat of all that are in the waters: you may eat all that have fins and scales" (Deuteronomy 14:6-9). Sheep, cow, goat. These are examples the Bible gives of animals who have a split hoof and chew the cud. These are examples of what Scripture calls "clean meat."

Pigs, rabbits, and camels are examples the Bible gives of animals unfit for human consumption. They have a purpose on earth, but God distinguished them from those animals He allowed for food. He warned, "Don't eat animals that don't have a split hoof *or* don't chew their cud."

During World War II Dr. David I. Macht reported in *The Hebrew Medical Journal* on a scientific experiment that involved injecting white mice with the muscle juices of a large variety of fish species as well as watching the growth of a certain plant seedling in a 1 percent solution of these same muscle juices. "The most interesting and surprising observation . . . was the fact that a toxin action was exerted by extracts from fishes having no scales while extracts of all those possessing them were found to be innocuous" ("An Experimental Appreciation of Leviticus XI. 9-12 and Deuteronomy XIV. 9-10," *The Hebrew Medical Journal*, 2, p. 166).

Any Bible student could have known that! God's instructions are clear: "And whatever does not have fins and scales you shall not eat; it is unclean for you" (Deuteronomy 14:10). Flounder, salmon, and tuna are acceptable to eat. Crabs, lobsters, and clams aren't.

God's first choice for His people is a vegetarian diet. There is an abundance of fruits, nuts, grains, and vegetables available to us today. A recent report in Newsweek declared that something called "phytochemicals" are the new frontier in cancer prevention research (Newsweek, Apr. 25, 1994). These anticancer agents aren't some new chemical cooked up in some scientist's pharmaceutical company. They're simply compounds found in a slice of tomato (tomatoes have 10,000 phytochemicals) or a bite of a cabbage. Broccoli, for instance, is loaded with these phytochemicals. Citrus fruits and berries contain powerful cancer fighters called flavenoids. They keep cancer-causing hormones from latching onto the cell.

Eat an abundance of fruits, grains, nuts, and vegetables. God's way! The healthy way! The life-giving way is a vegetarian diet.

Exercise. This is something the biblical characters didn't have to worry about. Hauling water from the village well, working in the gardens, and walking great distances took care of this health principle for them. Just the act of living was exercise enough.

But we live in a different generation. A generation of computer operators, truck drivers, secretaries, and administrators. A sedentary generation that needs consciously to work an exercise program into the weekly regime in order to increase the heartbeat, clear the head, and invigorate the mind. Doctors tell us that we should exercise a minimum of 20 minutes three times a week. The best way to get exercise is to find something enjoyable—and do it. Water aerobics, swimming, tennis, jogging, and walking are just a few examples. Make it an activity you look forward to, not something you dread.

I've recently taken up a new form of exercise—mountain biking. I not only benefit healthwise from this hobby, but I also relish the time spent with my son out in the mountains surrounding our California home.

Water. Humans can live much longer without food than they can without water. As a matter of fact, our bodies are composed of 65 to 70 percent water. Each day we lose approximately four pints. In order to replenish this, we need to drink six to eight glasses of water each day. That might sound like a lot, but I know people who have made it easier. They buy a gallon jug of water at the grocery store and set it beside their desk. By the 10:00 break they've had two glasses; by lunchtime they've had another two; by the 3:00 break, another two; by 5:00, another two. It's simply part of their daily routine.

Water is vital to the health of the body. It assists nature in resisting disease. It washes away impurities. It helps the body function more efficiently. Water is the drink of choice supplied by God for all His creatures.

Sunshine. Have you ever felt so stressed out that you took a little time off for a walk in the sunshine? Exercise wasn't the only thing that made you feel better. The sunlight served an important function as well.

In north Norway, where people experience only a few hours of sunlight in the winter, a new industry has cropped up—lightrooms in which people bask in artificial light simulating sunshine. And they have recorded marvelous results! Those who spent time in the sunlit rooms in winter were much less depressed than those who didn't. Endorphins in the brain are stimulated during times of exercise, especially outdoor exercise. They're closely related to our overall happiness and well-being. Some health professionals call exercise in the sunshine outdoors God's sedative. When their patients begin regular systematic outdoor exercise, there's a dramatic change in their outlook on life. They become more positive, more cheerful, and generally much more optimistic.

Physicians do warn us, however, of overexposure to sunlight. The ultraviolet rays can produce skin cancers. So if you do spend much time outside, you'd benefit by applying sunblock to those parts of your body exposed to the sun.

Temperance. Only once have I participated in a booze party. And to make the occasion even more memorable, it occurred after I'd been in the ministry a number of years, and several theology students were present to witness the event.

I'd been studying the Bible with Randy and his wife, Marian, for quite some time and had gotten to know them very well, or I never would have taken the liberty. We'd come to the lesson on healthful living, and although they were far from being alcoholics, social drinking was important to them. The thought of giving up alcohol completely was difficult for them. They were really struggling with the idea.

"All right," I said, "let's have a booze party here and now. Bring in everything you have."

Reluctantly they set their bottles of wine and hard liquor, along with a couple dozen cans of beer, on the kitchen table. I handed one to each of the theology students, the husband, and the wife. I picked up a bottle myself and said, "OK, unscrew the top." I could see the shock on the faces of the young students and the uncertainty on the faces of the couple.

"Very good," I said when they did as instructed. "Now, you, Randy, dump yours down the toilet. Marian, dump yours down the bathroom sink. Carl, dump yours down the kitchen sink. Ralph and I will dump ours down the toilet also!"

For a moment they stared at me in disbelief. Then we all broke into laughter, picked up a few bottles, and headed in different directions. It's been more than 20 years since I initiated the booze party. Recently Randy and Marian wrote me a letter and reminded me of the event. Today they're the successful owners of a motel, and they haven't touched a drop of alcohol since the night of that long-ago booze party!

Alcohol destroys brain cells immediately. Dr. Melvin

Knisely, of the University of South Carolina, invented a microscope with which he tested college students. By looking into the blood vessels of their eyes, he could tell how many drinks they'd had—two, six, eight, or more. The microscope allowed him to see the agglutination, or sticking together, of the blood cells. The more the oxygen supply is cut off, the more agglutination occurs. The greater the alcohol consumption, the greater the oxygen deprivation. We know, of course, that in an oxygen-starved brain, thousands of brain cells die.

Where does the Holy Spirit communicate with you? Through the brain, of course. That's why the enemy of God would love for you to consume alcohol. He'd love to cut off the means of communication between you and God. He'd love to weaken your inhibitions to evil. When people start drinking, they're apt to do things they wouldn't do otherwise. Say things. Take chances. Engage in sexual immorality.

Two out of five people who imbibe develop serious problems connected to the drinking. You don't know if you're that one of this minority until you lift that first glass. Two out of five doesn't seem like a bad statistic. But would you keep a dog who bit two out of five people? Of course not! The risk is too great! The Bible says: "Wine is a mocker, intoxicating drink arouses brawling, and whoever is led astray by it is not wise" (Proverbs 20:1). The only safe course when it comes to alcohol is complete avoidance. As long as you drink, you set a negative example for your family and friends. Their drinking problems may begin because of your influence.

And while we're on the subject of a temperate lifestyle, let's talk about smoking. America has finally acknowledged the dangers not only of smoking but also of secondhand smoke. Airlines, restaurants and other businesses, and governments have finally erected No Smoking signs in protection of those who choose health.

Years ago, before we had concrete evidence of the devastating results of smoking, it was one thing for a person to reach into a pack and light up. Today it's hardly imaginable that anyone would willingly endanger health by using tobacco. Cigarettes contain 29 poisons, and each one smoked takes 14½ minutes off one's life, according to the late Dr. Linus Pauling. Your chances of a heart attack are 250 times greater if you smoke. Your chances of incurring emphysema are 80 times greater if you smoke. The Bible says: "Thou shalt not kill" (Exodus 20:13, KJV). And God didn't just mean one person killing another. He also meant killing oneself.

Another aspect of a temperate lifestyle involves sexuality. I don't usually buy People magazine, but the cover of the October 24, 1994, issue compelled me to reach into my pocket and hand over the required $2.39. The cover read: "Special Report: Babies Who Have Babies. A day in the life of teen pregnancy in America." What I read in the article entitled "The Baby Trap" was pathetically sad.

It seems that the intemperate sexual lives of young Americans have escalated into what the magazine labeled "one of America's most urgent problems—teen pregnancy." More than 500,000 teenagers, many as young as 14, gave birth last year, according to the article. Now they struggle to finish high school, hold down a minimum-wage after-school job, and parent a child. On September 23, 1994, People sent out a team of 50 photographers and reporters to investigate.

Two things struck me about the dozen or so stories recounted in the People article. One was the fact that most of the young parents hoped that they could provide a better existence for their children than they had lived. Second, most were looking for love and security from another human being. The two things they desired most in life are probably the two things they're least likely to achieve. Most of the relationships were already terminated at the time of the magazine printing, and *People* indicated that one third of the daughters of teenage mothers will go on to become teen mothers themselves. In addition, other studies have indicated that couples who live together or experience sex before they marry are more likely to divorce than those who wait until the wedding night.

Despite the escalating occurrences of sexually transmitted diseases, despite the havoc wreaked on families because of extramarital affairs, despite the insecurity and destruction of self-esteem incurred in going from one partner to another, couples continue to violate God's principle of sex confined to marriage. Some people are swayed by popular songs, novels, movies, sitcoms, and advertisements that tout it's OK to do whatever you want with whomever you want.

A 17-year-old from the *People* article stated it rather succinctly: "Sex lasts for 15 minutes, which, compared to the rest of your life, isn't worth it. I made a mistake, and I'm going to have to live with it. But I won't have a normal life."

When it comes to temperance, God's way is always the best way.

Air. Even more crucial to survival than water is the need for air. We wouldn't live more than five or six minutes without it, yet we take this necessity for granted. Deep breaths of fresh air are important to good health. You'd do well to sleep with the windows open whenever possible. A brisk walk during the workday will do much to combat fatigue and drowsiness.

Rest. When God created Adam and Eve, He put them in the Garden of Eden to "tend and keep it" (Genesis 2: 15). God expects people to work. However, He's also a God of balance, and so He created a time of rest. "And on the seventh day God ended His work which He had done, and He rested on the seventh day from all His work which He had done" (verse 2).

We'll go into greater detail on the significance of the Sabbath in the next chapter, but it's important to note here that rest is part of God's plan for a healthy life. He didn't design us as a machine that could work 24 hours a day, seven days a week. In this generation especially, we need to be reminded that our bodies were designed with a requirement for "down time." Rest and rejuvenation are vital for optimal health.

We live in a fast-paced world of faxes, satellite television, high-speed cars, and a myriad of other inventions that lure us into believing we too can perform at that level. We cannot. God reminds us to stop each week and rest.

Trust. Fear is the opposite of trust, and fear is a crippler. It paralyzes the inflicted one from moving forward. It produces stress, and stress is linked to many of our diseases today.

The best way to combat fear is to remember that God is with you. He cares what happens to you, and He'll guide you if you let Him. It would do us all well to memorize the twenty-third psalm and recite it often:

"The Lord is my shepherd; I shall not want.

He maketh me to lie down in green pastures:

he leadeth me beside the still waters.

He restoreth my soul:

he leadeth me in the paths of righteousness for his name's sake.

Yea, though I walk through the valley of the shadow of death, I will fear no evil:

for thou art with me;

thy rod and thy staff they comfort me.

Thou preparest a table before me in the presence of mine enemies:

Thou anointest my head with oil;

my cup runneth over.

Surely goodness and mercy shall follow me all the days of my life:

and I will dwell in the house of the Lord for ever" (KJV).

Take God at His word. Put your hand in His hand and believe He'll guide you through the maze of life. Trust Him and see what a difference that will make.

A little boy sitting in the front row of one of my lectures watched night after night as I offered a rather energetic presentation. I walked back and forth across the platform and punctuated my points with gestures of the arms. One evening after watching me hook on a microphone that was connected to a long cord, he turned to his mother and asked, "Is that the cord they plug that guy into every night so that he has energy?"

No, I don't need to be plugged in to get energy. I just live by the eight natural remedies!

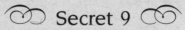
Rest Assured

C. Raymond Holmes was pastor of a 500-member Lutheran church in Michigan when he discovered a life-changing secret—an invitation from the heart of a loving heavenly Father to find rest and security. How? By renewing our tired minds and fatigued bodies as we soar like eagles into God's presence on the Sabbath.

God can surprise even pastors by the way He works. Sometimes He confronts us with truth. Shakes us up. Jars us from our complacency.

Ray Holmes pastored a 500-member Lutheran church in the upper peninsula of Michigan when his wife, Shirley, confronted him with the question of the seventh-day Sabbath. It's true that at times he'd felt uncomfortable in his denomination. He wasn't in harmony with those who believed that the concrete teachings of the Bible needed to be updated. There was a longing in his heart to base his faith on biblical truth, on a faithful commitment to Scripture. But the seventh-day Sabbath? It wasn't possible that so many leading scholars could be wrong!

Pastor Holmes was committed to the supremacy of Scripture in his own life. His attitude was "If God's Word says it, I believe it." His faith was built on the solid truths of God's Word. But this time he was shaken to the core. He'd been brought up from childhood in his denomination's tradition of keeping the first day. He'd assumed that since Christ rose from the dead on the first day that the true Bible Sabbath was indeed Sunday, the first day of the week.

Responding to his wife's challenge regarding the Sabbath, Pastor Holmes pored through the Bible in an attempt to unravel the truth. Ultimately his discovery led him to resign his position as pastor of the Lutheran congregation and become a Sabbathkeeper. Pastor Holmes discovered that illusive truth that the majority isn't always right.

✦

There was a time that prominent scientists believed that the world was flat. There was a time that intelligent people believed that the earth was the center of the universe. There was a time that health-care practitioners believed that inhaling tobacco smoke was good for the lungs. Corporate belief by a large body of people doesn't make something true.

As we delve into our study of the seventh-day Sabbath, keep an open mind. Don't take my word for it. Rather, analyze the evidence. Scrutinize the Scriptures. Ask "What is the Bible saying?" And be honest with yourself. God may have a surprise for you as He did for Pastor Holmes—a surprise package that will deliver sweet inner peace. A rest assured.

The first record of the Sabbath in Scripture is found in Genesis 2:1-3, at the close of Creation week. "Thus the heavens and the earth, and all the host of them, were finished. And on the seventh day God ended His work which He had done, and He rested on the seventh day from all His work which He had done. Then God blessed the seventh day and sanctified it, because in it He rested from all His work which God had created and made."

After carefully fashioning the earth in six days, God rested on the seventh day. He took a break from His work. Why? Was He tired? Hardly. On that first Sabbath God rested because of a perfect sense of fulfillment. He'd done everything possible to ensure Adam's and Eve's happiness. He rested with the joyful anticipation of an intimate relationship with the creatures He'd made. By resting on the seventh day, God was setting an example for Adam and Eve. He planned a celebration for them—a day on which they stopped their work routine and rested and worshiped. As the recently published *Catechism of the Catholic Church* (1994), which became an overnight best-seller, so rightly states: "God's action is the model for human action. If God 'rested' . . . on the seventh day, man too ought to 'rest'" (2172).

The Sabbath is also included in the only document recorded directly by God's hand, the Ten Commandments. Note the fourth commandment: "Remember the Sabbath day, to keep it holy. Six days you shall labor and do all your work, but the seventh day is the Sabbath of the Lord your God. In it you shall do no work: you, nor your son, nor your daughter, nor your manservant, nor your maidservant, nor your cattle, nor your stranger who is within your gates. For in six days the Lord made the heavens and the earth, the sea, and all that is in them, and rested the seventh day. Therefore the Lord blessed the Sabbath day and hallowed it" (Exodus 20:8-11).

Again the new *Catechism of the Catholic Church* says: "The sabbath is at the heart of Israel's law" (348). It was a perpetual reminder of His supreme authority and creative power. It's a memorial of Creation. Again the latest catechism, featuring a special introductory message by Pope John Paul II, properly observes that "in speaking of the sabbath Scripture recalls creation" (2169). In our modern age in which science speaks of evolution as proven fact, the Sabbath calls us back to the worship of our Creator. It's a weekly remembrance of the loving God who formed us from the dust of the ground and breathed into us the breath of life. We're not merely a random collection of chemicals combined by chance. God made us! We're created in His image! And each week we have the opportunity to rest our tired minds and exhausted bodies and unite with the One who is responsible for our existence.

Furthermore, the Sabbath is a·call to spend time with our families. It's possible to become so busy during the week that family members hardly see each other. In some cases meaningful dialogue is nonexistent. One study indicates that the average American father spends less than one hour per week in personal communication alone with his children. However, the Sabbath is a time set aside by God for families to commune with Him and with each other.

The Sabbath brings a sense of security to all of life. It's a reference point in the week. It constantly reminds us that a loving Creator cares for us more than we can imagine.

God established the Sabbath as a sign between Himself and His people. "Moreover I also gave them My Sabbaths, to be a sign between them and Me, that they might know that I am the Lord who sanctifies them" (Ezekiel 20: 12). "Hallow My Sabbaths, and they will be a sign between Me and you, that you may know that I am the Lord your God" (verse 20).

I've met people who have said, "One day is as good as the next. It really doesn't make much difference which day you keep, as long as you keep one in seven." Yet notice the clear teaching of the Bible. Which day did God sanctify? The seventh day. In six days He worked—He created His masterpiece—then He rested. He established a memorial of His great work, and then He sanctified it as a "sign between Me and you, that you may know that I am the Lord your God."

If it's important to God, certainly it should be important also to you, should it not? God is interested in your physical, mental, emotional, and spiritual health. Each seventh day He personally invites you into His palace in time to renew your tired mind and fatigued body. The Sabbath provides the spiritual glue for a bonding experience with your heavenly Father. This weekly fellowship will recharge your spiritual batteries and lift your spirits. On Sabbath you can soar like an eagle into God's presence.

Jesus Himself faithfully kept the Sabbath, as the 1994 Catholic catechism emphasizes: "Jesus never fails to respect the holiness of this day [the seventh-day Sabbath]. . . . The sabbath is the day of the Lord of mercies and a day to honor God" (2174). Luke reports: "So He came to Nazareth, where He had been brought up. And as His custom was, He went into the synagogue on the Sabbath day, and stood up to read" (Luke 4:16).

The biblical record indicates that God was particular about the Sabbath from the moment of Creation. He sanctified it. He regarded it as a sign between Himself and His people. If He'd decided to alter His covenant, certainly Jesus would have known. He would have mentioned it during His lifetime. He would have given us some clue, at least a hint of a change. Yet during His 33 years on this earth Jesus regularly observed the Sabbath. He never mentioned a change.

Even the events surrounding Jesus' death on the cross were woven around the Sabbath hours. "That day was the Preparation, and the Sabbath drew near. And the women who had come with Him from Galilee followed after, and they observed the tomb and how His body was laid. Then they returned and prepared spices and fragrant oils. And they rested on the Sabbath according to the commandment. Now on the first day of the week, very early in the morning, they, and certain other women with them, came to the tomb bringing the spices which they had prepared" (Luke 23:54-24:1).

The Christian world is basically united as to which day Christ died. We call it Good Friday. And what about the day Christ arose? No problem identifying it. Christians around the world celebrate Easter Sunday. So the three days in succession are: the day Christ died, Friday; the day Christ was in the tomb, Sabbath; and the day He arose, Sunday. The Sabbath is the day between Friday and Sunday, or the day we now call Saturday.

As a matter of fact, Jesus mentioned the Sabbath when He discussed the destruction of Jerusalem, an event that would take place in A.D. 70, approximately 40 years after His death. "And pray that your flight may not be in winter or on the Sabbath" (Matthew 24:20). This would suggest that Jesus didn't anticipate any change in the Sabbath after He returned to His Father in heaven.

Paul, the apostle to the Gentiles, kept the Sabbath. "And when the Jews went out of the synagogue, the Gentiles begged that these words might be preached to them the next Sabbath. . . . And the next Sabbath almost the whole city came together to hear the word of God" (Acts 13:42-44). Here we read that the early Christians, "almost the whole city," came together on the Sabbath day. So the commandment was still in effect after the cross, even during the early days of Christianity.

Because Isaiah clearly prophesied that the Sabbath would be kept during the great restoration of God's people, we can infer that the Bible indicates that Sabbath observance will continue right into eternity. " 'And it shall come to pass that from one New Moon to another, and from one Sabbath to another, all flesh shall come to worship before Me,' says the Lord" (Isaiah 66:23).

I expect to be surprised in heaven. Surprised by the magnificence, surprised by the beauty, surprised by what Jesus has prepared. But worship on the seventh day won't come as a surprise. God established this practice at Creation. In the Ten Commandments He reminded us to keep the Sabbath. Jesus Himself observed the seventh day. Early Christians worshiped on the Sabbath. And I infer from Scripture that the practice will continue right into eternity.

Until then God invites you and me to find rest each Sabbath in His loving presence—respite for our frayed nerves and restless anxiety, as well as from life's deepest tragedies.

✦

Lisa lived on the beautiful island of Oahu in Hawaii. Living on the island paradise was a dream. A dream until one morning her husband said, "Honey, I'm going for a hike"—and never returned. Alone during the early morning in an isolated mountainous region along a volcanic ridge, Hank slipped. The loose gravel gave way beneath his feet. He plunged headlong into a 500-foot ravine, broke his neck, and died. It took the authorities three days to find him.

Lisa had a hard time getting over her loss. She wept. She grieved. She mourned. Even with the passing of weeks and months, it still hurt. And as Lisa worked through her pain, she heard the call of Another: "Come to Me, all you who labor and are heavy laden, and I will give you rest" (Matthew 11:28).

Lisa had been brought up as a child to keep the Bible Sabbath. And as she sensed God's call to her heart, she now believed that only by returning to her roots could she find rest. To Lisa keeping the seventh-day Sabbath symbolized resting in God's loving arms. Resting from her care. Resting from her anxiety. Resting from her burdens. Resting from her troubled heart.

Each week a palace in time descends from heaven to earth. God opens the door and invites you to enter into His rest. Sabbath symbolizes that there's a place in God's heart for you to find rest from the cares, perplexities, and worries of life.

The Sabbath isn't a legalistic requirement. It isn't a cumbersome burden. It's an invitation from the heart of a loving heavenly Father for you to find rest and security in Him.

I haven't always observed the Sabbath. As a matter of fact, I spent my youth in parochial schools and as an altar boy, known by name in the rectory. But when the truth was presented to me, when I heard God's call, when I analyzed the evidence, I felt I had to follow God's will. I immediately responded and turned my life over to the Creator of the seventh-day Sabbath.

In the next chapter I'll tell you my experience in learning about the Sabbath, about seeking guidance from my priest, and how I, along with millions the world around, followed a tradition set up by people (not God) long after Christ's death.

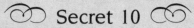

The Question My Priest Couldn't Answer

Mark Finley, altar boy and president-elect of the local Catholic youth group at St. Patrick's Cathedral, asked his priest a simple question: "Why do we go to church on Sunday?" Mark's probing mind had discovered in Scripture a life-changing secret about Sunday.

As I grew older, I began to wonder why my dad went to church on Saturdays. When he was baptized into the Seventh-day Adventist Church, he'd promised my mother that he'd never impose his beliefs on the children. And he kept that promise. I grew up respecting Dad for the stable, Christian man that he was, but I didn't understand his religious beliefs.

On Friday nights the sliding doors between the living room and parlor in our old colonial home were closed. On one side of those doors Dad quietly studied his Bible by the light of a table lamp. On the other side of the doors my mom, three sisters, and I watched *Mr. Ed*, *Ozzie and Harriet*, and other television shows popular at the time. We made sure the volume was turned low so as not to disturb Dad.

However, I rather liked the peaceful atmosphere in the parlor with Dad, and sometimes on Friday nights I'd join him there. But why? Why did he begin his time of worship on Friday night?

We offered our thanks to the same God at mealtime, requested protection from the same God at bedtime, and remembered the same Baby Jesus at Christmastime. But weekends were different. Dad walked one mile to the Adventist church on Saturday, and on Sunday the rest of us crossed the street to Saint Patrick's Cathedral.

By the summer before I started college, I could wonder no longer. I had to know. "Why do you go to church on Saturday?" I asked one day, and Dad agreed to explain. He showed me what the Bible has to say about the Sabbath, that God declared the seventh day holy, that it serves as a memorial to Creation and redemption, and that it continues as a sign of allegiance to God.

The texts seemed pretty clear to me, but I was no Bible expert. I decided to question my priest about it. I'd attended Catholic schools, served as an altar boy with the priests for five years, and was about to be voted as president of the local Catholic youth organization. Our parish priest was a good friend. He responded to my knock on the door and graciously welcomed me.

"Father," I said, "I have a question about one of our doctrines."

"Have a seat," he answered with a smile. "I'd be pleased to help."

"It's the Sabbath commandment," I said and began to repeat the text in Exodus 20.

"Yes, I know the text," he said. "What's your question?"

I took a deep breath and asked, "If the Bible says to worship on the seventh day, why do we go to church on Sunday, the first day of the week?"

The priest stared at me a moment. He seemed rather incredulous that a teenager would even think to ask such a question. "My son," he said, "you don't treat the Bible as a set of isolated verses; you treat it as a whole. There are texts in the New Testament that make the Sabbath problem perfectly clear."

I mustered up the courage to tell him that I'd studied the New Testament, too. All I could find on the subject were references to Jesus' attendance at synagogue on Sabbath, Paul's observing the Sabbath, and John's reference to the Lord's day. My voice sort of trailed off. I feared that perhaps I'd overstepped my bounds. I paused a moment, then asked if he could get a Bible and help me understand certain verses.

The priest rose quickly and went out of the room. Several minutes later he returned empty-handed. "I can't seem to find a Bible. But if you come back sometime, I'm sure we can get things straightened out."

I've never been able to forget those words. At that moment I realized that deciding who was more worthy of my attention—someone who had searched God's Word earnestly in order to find out what he must do, or someone who couldn't find a Bible in the rectory—would be easy.

I'm sure that priest was an exception. But unfortunately, he represents a tragic failing among religious leaders of every denomination. Some of them bend the truth because they don't stand on God's Word. They're not shaped by God's truth, because they've lost their grip on the solid rock of divine principles. In short, they've misplaced their Bibles. If the Bible isn't the center of the rectory, the center of the church, the center of the home, there's a problem. How can it shape lives and renew minds if it's hidden in a corner somewhere?

Instead of trying to manipulate the truth to serve our own ends, we need to imitate the spirit of David. "The law of the Lord is perfect, converting the soul; the testimony of the Lord is sure, making wise the simple; the statutes of the Lord are right, rejoicing the heart; the commandment of the Lord is pure, enlightening the eyes" (Psalm 19:7, 8).

✦

Why have the majority of Christians come to worship on Sunday? Why do they consider it holy? You can search all day, but you won't find one reference to God's sanctifying Sunday in the Bible. You won't uncover one reference to a change in the day of worship, whether you explore the Old Testament or the New Testament. On the contrary, Jesus explained that He did *not* come to change the law. "Do not think that I came to destroy the Law or the Prophets. I did not come to destroy but to fulfill. For assuredly, I say to you, till heaven and earth pass away, one jot or one tittle will by no means pass from the law till all is fulfilled. Whoever therefore breaks one of the least of these commandments, and teaches men so, shall be called least in the kingdom of heaven; but whoever does and teaches them, he shall be called great in the kingdom of heaven" (Matthew 5:17-19).

Jesus didn't destroy the law. Jesus didn't change the Sabbath. As a matter of fact, in verse 19 He makes a pretty strong indictment against those who teach people to break one of His commandments, including the Sabbath commandment. So what's the origin of this common practice, if it isn't the Son of God?

Before I answer that question, I'd like to tell you one of my favorite stories. In worshiping on Sunday, Christians are very much like a certain sentry in Russia who guarded a particular shrub in the czar's beautiful garden.

One day during the time of imperial Russia, the czar was walking through one of the parks connected with his palace and came upon a sentry standing guard near a patch of shrubs. Surprised to find a guard in that place, he inquired, "What are you doing?"

"I don't know," answered the sentry. "I'm following the captain's orders."

The czar asked the captain, "Why do you have a sentry standing guard over a patch of shrubs?"

"Regulations have always been that way," the captain responded, "but I don't know the reason for it."

After a thorough investigation, the czar discovered that nobody in his court could remember a time when it had been done any other way. So the czar turned to the archives containing the ancient records, and to his surprise he discovered that 100 years earlier Catherine the Great had ordered a rosebush to be planted and had stationed a sentry nearby so that no one would trample the young plant. The rosebush had long since died, of course. Yet a guard continued to stand watching. But he didn't know why.

And that's what scores of people in Christian churches are doing today—defending a doctrine that's slipped into the church through tradition, a doctrine that's a myth and not a command of God.

✦

A study of history reveals that the Christian church continued to worship on the Sabbath until the end of the first century. But early in the second century some Christians voluntarily began celebrating the Crucifixion weekend. They centered their celebrations on the Crucifixion day, which coincided with the Jewish Passover. But because of a series of Jewish revolts against the Romans, the Jews became more and more unpopular in the empire, and Christians began to suffer because people regarded them as a Jewish sect. Celebration of the Passover in memory of the Crucifixion was seen by many as further identifying Christianity with Judaism. As a result, some of the Christians decided to make a change.

It was Sixtus, the bishop of the Christian church in Rome, who most likely began the process that led to a transference of the day of worship from Sabbath to Sunday. He convinced Christians to celebrate the Resurrection, which occurred on Sunday. At first the celebration was not a weekly observance but an annual one. And by changing the celebration to Sunday and applying it to the Resurrection, the Christians in Rome were able to disassociate themselves from the Jews.

It just so happened that this Resurrection celebration coincided with a joyous Roman festival in honor of the sun. The converted sun worshiper felt very much at home with the Christian spring festival, held on the sun's day, to honor the Resurrection. Thus Sixtus, by encouraging Christians to celebrate the Resurrection on the first day, actually put them in the position of worshiping on the sun's day.

The next important act in the drama came near the end of the second century, when Pope Victor sought to enforce the annual observance of Resurrection Sunday. He ordered all bishops excommunicated who wouldn't follow the plan of celebrating the Resurrection festival. This decree enforcing Sunday observance was his attempt to gain control of the church. Rome's Socrates, the skilled church historian (not the Greek philosopher who had lived many centuries earlier), would later write: "Although almost all churches throughout the world celebrate the sacred mysteries on the sabbath of every week, yet the Christians of Alexandria and at Rome, on account of some ancient tradition, have ceased to do this" (*Ecclesiastical History*, book 5, chap. 22, trans. in *Nicene and Post-Nicene Fathers*, 2nd series, vol. 2, p. 132).

The first law actually commanding Sunday rest was issued by the emperor Constantine in A.D. 321. His decree declared: "On the venerable Day of the Sun let the magistrates and people residing in cities rest, and let all workshops be closed. In the country, however, persons engaged in agriculture may freely and lawfully continue their pursuits" (Codex Justinianus, I. iii., tit. 12, 3, trans. in Philip Schaff, *History of the Christian Church*, 5th edition, vol. 3, p. 380, note 1).

But church historian Philip Schaff makes this significant point: "The Sunday law of Constantine must not be overrated. . . . There is no reference whatever in his law either to the fourth commandment or to the resurrection of Christ. Besides he expressly exempted the country districts. . . . Christians and pagans had been accustomed to festival rests; Constantine made these rests to synchronize, and gave the preference to Sunday" (*History of the Christian Church*, vol. 3, p. 380).

Thousands of years earlier the prophet Daniel had predicted an attempt to change God's law. "He shall speak pompous words against the Most High, shall persecute the saints of the Most High, and shall intend to change times and law. Then the saints shall be given into his hand for a time and times and half a time" (Daniel 7:25).

It's important to note that Daniel says that "he shall *intend* to change times and law." He doesn't say that the laws will, in fact, be changed, only that an authority figure will attempt to do so. He will, of course, think that he has changed them.

But those who study the Bible and history won't be fooled. They'll understand the significance of a change in the day of worship. God instituted the celebration of the Sabbath day at Creation as a memorial of His creative power. As we discovered in the previous chapter, Ezekiel reminds us that observance of the Sabbath indicates our allegiance to God. We must, therefore, conclude that worship on another day indicates allegiance to another power.

Paul predicted that apostasy would creep into the early church. "Therefore take heed to yourselves and to all the flock, among which the Holy Spirit has made you overseers, to shepherd the church of God which He purchased with His own blood. For I know this, that after my departure savage wolves will come in among you, not sparing the flock. Also from among yourselves men will rise up, speaking perverse things, to draw away the disciples after themselves" (Acts 20:28-31).

At the end of his life Paul wanted to leave the followers of Christ with a few last words. He reminded them that Christ has bought the church with His own blood and that it was their responsibility to feed the flock. But from among themselves—followers within the church—as well as from wolves without, he warned them to take heed.

If you had to be careful of only the wolves, wouldn't life be easier? The wolves are easier to spot. When apostasy occurs from within an organization, it's more difficult to detect. We don't want to believe within our hearts that those we love and respect or those who think of themselves as God's messengers are the very ones who have broken God's law and are teaching others to do likewise. As sad as it may be, the truth is the truth. And the question becomes Now that we know, what do we do? Continue on as though we don't know, or follow God's will?

✦

What does the church say about its role in the change of the Sabbath? Does it agree or disagree? The Roman Catholic Church sees in the change of the Sabbath a sign of its power. Statements made by Catholic authorities show this clearly.

On page 174 of A *Doctrinal Catechism*, Catholic writer Stephen Keenan asks the question: *"Have you any other way of proving that the church has power to institute festivals of precept?"* He provides this answer: "Had she not such power, she could not have done that in which all modern religionists agree with her—she could not have substituted the observance of Sunday, the first day of the week, for the observance of Saturday, the seventh day, a change for which there is no scriptural authority."

Another Catholic writer, Monsignor Louis Segur, has this to say: "It was the Catholic Church which, by the authority of Jesus Christ, has transferred this rest to the Sunday in remembrance of the resurrection of our Lord. Thus the observance of *Sunday* by the Protestants is an homage they pay, in spite of themselves, to the authority of the [Catholic] Church" (*Plain Talk About the Protestantism of Today*, p. 213).

It isn't my intent to engage in mudslinging against the

denomination in which I was raised. Actually, I owe much to that church. The priests and nuns awakened in me a yearning for spiritual awareness. It is from them that I learned to love the Lord. On the other hand, I don't want to guard a shrub where a rosebush once bloomed. For me it's essential to know the truth as the Bible and history bear it out. And once I've learned that truth, I must align myself with it.

Transition points are always the most difficult in life. If you've done something a certain way for years, it may seem impossible to envision completing that task another way. But what if you learned that that other way was the original intent, that in that other way your Creator had planted a blessing? that in fact there was a hidden story that you didn't know before? Would it make a difference to you then?

✦

Throughout the ages there have always been people who've understood the importance of Sabbath worship. They've cherished this truth and passed it from generation to generation.

Oswald Glait was one such man. He repeatedly risked his life for the Sabbath truth. He was captured in 1545 while on an evangelistic mission in central Europe. After a year and six weeks in jail he awakened at midnight to the thunderous footsteps of soldiers marching down the hall to his cell. These cruel mercenaries bound him hand and foot, dragged him through the city, and cast him into the Danube.

Little did they realize that the truth he gave his life for, like the ripples created by a rock thrown into a clean pond on a tranquil evening, would rapidly spread throughout central Europe. This truth about the biblical Sabbath spread to Great Britain and Scandinavia and was later transferred to America. For many an early Sabbathkeeping Christian, the Lord of the Sabbath was worth dying for.

Oswald Glait's witness for truth speaks eloquently to us today. His courage testifies of God's power. His blood symbolically cries out through the ages: "Don't ever compromise truth!"

The words of Scripture proclaim: "Sanctify them by Your truth. Your word is truth" (John 17:17). If you're serious about learning the truth, turn to God's Word. Within its pages the truth has been preserved.

Economic Survival in Tough Times

The national debt is so immense that if the government were an individual citizen it would long ago have filed for bankruptcy. Maybe you have so many bills and so little discretionary income that you suspect the expression *financial security* is a contradiction of terms. Perhaps you need, then, to learn the biblical secret to financial security. It just might change your life.

The door to my study in the small New England church I pastored swung open to reveal a church member who was rather distraught. He shut the door behind him and looked me straight in the eye before he spoke. "Pastor, I'm angry. Last week you preached a sermon on returning a faithful tithe to the Lord, so I've brought you my bills." At that he produced a wrinkled paper bag, pulled out receipts one by one, and threw them on my desk.

"Here's my apartment rent stub," he said. "Here's my food bill. Here's my electric bill. Here's what I pay for my car payment and gasoline each week. Pastor, you say I have to pay tithe on top of all this? You say I have to return money to God? My bills are higher than my income. How can I possibly do it? It's simply not feasible." He crossed his arms and looked down at me triumphantly.

I looked up at him from my desk and smiled. "Ben, by the method you're using, you're correct. It *is* impossible. Totally impossible. But Ben, I have a question for you. Has that method brought you financial freedom? Has it gotten you out of debt? If not, why not try God's method as an experiment? What do you have to lose? You're already in debt. Try it for three months and see what happens. God doesn't need your money, Ben. But *you* need God's blessing with your finances!"

✦

I couldn't argue with Ben on one point. We do live in tough economic times. For many it's difficult just to meet expenses. A lot of people have very little discretionary income. Although their income has inched ahead, their expenses have taken a giant step forward. In some areas of the country costs for just the basics—housing, health care, food, and clothing—stretch families to the limit. That's exactly why we need God as a partner in our finances.

God gives each one the ability to acquire wealth. "And you shall remember the Lord your God, for it is He who gives you power to get wealth, that He may establish His covenant which He swore to your fathers, as it is this day" (Deuteronomy 8:18). Without your God-given abilities you'd be unable to attain wealth at all. Everything belongs to Him, and it's only as He blesses you with health, talents, and opportunities that you're able to work and earn money at all.

Because God's blessings surround you, have you taken them for granted? It might be good to remember to whom all things belong. "The earth is the Lord's, and all its fullness, the world and those who dwell therein. For He has founded it upon the seas, and established it upon the waters" (Psalm 24:1, 2).

That which all of us take for granted—the sun to warm us and grow our food, the water we drink and bathe in, even the gravity to keep us on this earth—were all put into place by a living, all-powerful Creator for our benefit. God

99

thought of every detail we'd need to survive, and He made sure it was in place before we were created. The earth is His. He has created it. He owns it, but freely shares its bounties with us.

To remind you and me that all the good things of life do come from Him, He asks us to return a tithe to Him. And when we do, He's promised to bless us further. " 'Bring all the tithes into the storehouse, that there may be food in My house, and prove Me now in this,' says the Lord of hosts, 'if I will not open for you the windows of heaven and pour out for you such blessing that there will not be room enough to receive it' " (Malachi 3:10).

The biblical book of Leviticus explains the meaning of the word "tithe." "Concerning the tithe of the herd or the flock, of whatever passes under the rod, the tenth one shall be holy to the Lord" (Leviticus 27:32).

A tithe, therefore, is one tenth of your increase. Just as the Lord asks for a percentage of your time, one seventh, so He asks for a percentage of your increase.

God doesn't need your money, of course. What He does need is your trust, and that's what the tithing system is all about. When you trust God enough to put Him first in your life, in your time, in your financial planning, and with your energies, He'll open the windows of heaven. He'll bless your life in ways that now seem impossible.

✦

Yes, you might agree with Ben that you can't afford to pay tithe. Personally, I believe I can't afford *not* to return a tenth to God. I'd rather have nine tenths of my income with God's blessing than ten tenths without His blessing. His blessing is worth more to me than one tenth of my income.

When God created Adam and Eve, He told them about the tree of knowledge of good and evil, which He placed in the Garden of Eden as a test of their loyalty to Him. After they sinned and were banished from the garden, He could no longer test their faithfulness in that way. So at some point He instituted the tithing system as a similar test. It's something He required of His children in order that they might demonstrate their trust in Him.

Tithing is a proportional giving system. The more you have, the more you're asked to return. God doesn't ask that you put $50 or $100 in the offering plate every week regardless of your earnings. He asks, instead, that you return only 10 percent of your increase. The dollar figure is according to how you've been blessed.

So you're having trouble with your finances and think you can't afford to pay tithe? Why not include God as your financial partner and see what He'll do? We all need to return a tithe to God, but in actuality the time you most need to include tithe in your monthly budget is when you can least afford it—when you need God's blessing the most.

When you regularly return a tithe to God you're essentially saying "God, come into my life. I want You to be in charge of all aspects of my life. I don't want any part of my life untouched by Your power." On the other hand, if you fail to return a faithful tithe, you're in effect saying "Leave me alone, God. I don't want Your help. I can manage my finances on my own."

I believe that Jesus diagnosed the essence of the problem: "Take heed and beware of covetousness, for one's life does not consist in the abundance of the things he possesses" (Luke 12:15).

What's Jesus saying here? Your life, your worth, isn't made up of what you possess. So beware of greed. Why? Because it's a dead end. You can never get enough. You can never possess enough things to feel secure. You have to look elsewhere to become a secure human being.

Money becomes addictive for those who use it to try to get security. Paul wrote to Timothy about the danger of the rich placing their hope in their wealth. The Bible says that the *love* of money is the root of all evil. And Jesus urged His followers to lay up treasures in heaven. "For where your treasure is, there your heart will be also" (Matthew 6:21).

Do you see what Jesus was getting at? It's a question of security. Trying to store up treasure on earth will never fill up your heart. Jesus knew that the only way you can fill your heart is by investing in heavenly values.

Investors during the 1920s, the Roaring Twenties, thought they were amassing treasures on earth. The stock market just kept going up, up, up. Fortunes could be made overnight, it seemed.

But then came that fateful crash on October 29, 1929. The bottom fell out of the stock market. And investors who a few hours before had been flying sky-high were jumping out of buildings.

It was all over. Their security was gone.

After the Great Depression the U.S. government created a variety of safeguards for the stock market. Insurance and financial regulations were designed to prevent another disaster like the crash of '29.

And so during the eighties the market began to grow red hot. Stock prices kept going up, up, up. People were making fortunes overnight, it seemed. Junk bond trading and corporate takeovers were all the rage.

But then came October 19, 1987. The bubble burst, and prices nose-dived. Stocks plunged 508 points in one day. An entire year's spectacular gains were wiped out.

What many people don't realize is that the crash of '87 was actually steeper than the crash of '29. In 1929 the Dow lost 12.9 percent of its value. In 1987 the Dow lost 22.6 percent of its value—$500 million in paper value simply vanished into thin air.

I'd like you to notice a description of this kind of financial disaster—a description written centuries ago in the New Testament book of James. "Come now, you rich, weep and howl for your miseries that are coming upon you! Your riches are corrupted, and your garments are moth-eaten. Your gold and silver are corroded, and their corrosion will be a witness against you and will eat your flesh like fire. You have heaped up treasure in the last days" (James 5:1-3).

James says that gold and silver can be corrupted, savings eroded. Now, that doesn't seem very likely, does it? After all, you can store gold away for centuries. But what about the gold and silver of the stock market? The gold and silver of leveraged buyouts and junk bonds and Swiss bank accounts? As we've seen, those can disappear into thin air, corroded away by the whims of the market. And to those who lose fortunes I'm sure it does seem that these lost riches are eating their flesh like fire.

Human finances are inherently insecure. Windfall profits are always a few steps away from vanishing into thin air.

How can anyone even use the term *financial security* in the United States when the federal government labors under a debt of some $4 trillion? That's how far the country is in the hole. Just paying interest on that debt eats up billions of dollars a year. In fact, about 20 percent of your taxes goes to pay interest on America's public debt.

The term *financial security* is an oxymoron, a contradiction in terms. You never have quite enough in the bank, quite enough securely invested. After all, where will interest rates go next month, next year? How will the economy hold up? When you get right down to it, there's no such thing as financial security. If it's financial, it's not security.

Yes, we try to invest our money as best we can. Yes, we try to save for our kids' college education or for retirement. But all that will never create real security. It won't create a real island of peace and safety. Financial security is a myth, period.

Sooner or later materialism dries us up and hardens us like concrete pavement, where nothing can grow. We need an alternative. We need the Living Rock in our lives.

We need the Solid Rock as the center of our attention.

Jesus Christ is the source of real security. His voice alone is more piercing and compelling than all the cries on the stock market floor. He alone is big enough on the horizon to stand above the tallest towers of the metropolis. He alone, the eternal Creator, is mighty enough to hold us up when all the foundations are quaking and shattering.

But the biggest reason that Jesus can provide ultimate security is simply this: He fills up human hearts. He can meet your deepest needs. You don't need to go on trying to get more and more things, because with Christ you no longer have holes in your heart.

Christ, the Solid Rock, has enough leverage to move human nature, to overturn greed, to awaken slumbering spirituality. His perfect life, His death on the cross, His offer of pardon and power—they make Him the Solid Rock you can rely on.

Wrestling in the Baptistry

Boris, martial arts master and marathoner, slipped from his watchtower while on a KGB assignment. During his hospitalization he learned a secret about a "mountain sermon" that could change your life as it did his.

Rhea was insistent. "Pastor, I've come to this church to be baptized, and you *will* baptize me today. I won't take no for an answer."

Normally a pastor is delighted when someone requests baptism. I certainly am. We were planning to baptize almost 100 people in a Honolulu Adventist church that day, and I was rejoicing with every one of them. But Rhea's situation was different. Her ideas regarding Jesus were distorted. She had little knowledge of Bible truth and had strong cult tendencies. She was confused on the very basics of Christianity. In good conscience I couldn't baptize her into a Christ whose truth she didn't know.

I gently shared my willingness to arrange weekly Bible studies to explain the gospel. Kindly I attempted to reassure her of our interest in her and our commitment to see her grow in Christ. "Rhea, I'll be delighted to baptize you once we've studied together," I told her graciously. "Once you understand the significance of Bible baptism."

Her penetrating brown eyes never wavered from mine, and she replied in a strong, not-to-be-argued-with voice, "Either you baptize me today or else."

"Or else what, Rhea?"

"Or else this." Shouting to the congregation that I was a fraud and hypocrite, Rhea shot past me onto the platform and dived into the baptismal pool. She went down once and came up. Two times. Three times.

The scene would have been worse if the organist hadn't been alert and opened up the bellows full blast! Those in the rear of the congregation sang along lustily, while those in the front gaped in astonishment.

Seven times, eight times, nine times. Rhea baptized herself 10 times as a substitute for her dead relatives before four strong Samoan men wrestled her out of the baptistry.

✦

What's the meaning of the biblical practice of baptism? Why was I reluctant to baptize Rhea? Is there magic water in the pool that saves you? How was Jesus baptized, and what does this signify? Why be baptized at all? Is it just a form, a meaningless ritual? Let's study the Bible and find out.

After Jesus had risen from the dead, He appeared to His followers on several occasions. The very last conversation that Matthew records Jesus having had with the disciples includes the subject of baptism. "Go therefore and make disciples of all the nations, baptizing them in the name of the Father and of the Son and of the Holy Spirit, teaching them to observe all things that I have commanded you; and lo, I am with you always, even to the end of the age" (Matthew 28:19, 20).

Just before Jesus ascended into heaven He instructed the disciples to spread the gospel to all nations. He told them to teach the whole world what He'd taught them. And part of that command included baptism. "Make disciples of all the nations," said Jesus, and then His followers were to baptize these new disciples "in the name of the Father and of the Son and of the Holy Spirit."

Jesus had spent three and a half years living with and teaching His disciples. And now when He was about to leave them, He had a few last words. Now, the last words someone chooses to say are usually very important—a culmination of what has been on the heart for a long time, a condensing of what has been said all along. For Jesus, the subject was baptism.

The gospel of Mark records the same story with the addition of these few lines: "He who believes and is baptized will be saved" (Mark 16:16). Baptism, then, is an outward sign of belief. It signifies that the new Christian has analyzed the Word, internalized the Word, responded to the Word, and has chosen to follow the Word. Baptism is a visible response of what's happening in the heart of the believer. And Mark's gospel indicates it's tied to salvation.

The disciples took Jesus' charge seriously. The book of Acts records numerous accounts of their preaching and baptizing new believers. At one point when Peter was preaching, the crowd was touched and asked what they needed to do in response. Peter replied: "Repent, and let every one of you be baptized in the name of Jesus Christ for the remission of sins; and you shall receive the gift of the Holy Spirit" (Acts 2:38).

Repentance is a prerequisite to baptism. In order to be baptized, one must first renounce sin. The act would have no significance if the one being baptized continued in the same sinful manner as before. Baptism marks true repentance. It's a new beginning. It signifies an inner cleansing—the washing away of sin. We are then promised pardon in the name of Jesus Christ.

As a gift at this ceremony, Jesus has promised to send the Holy Spirit. The Comforter. The Guide.

Baptism is symbolic of resurrection. Romans 6:4 says: "Therefore we were buried with Him through baptism into death, that just as Christ was raised from the dead by the glory of the Father, even so we also should walk in newness of life." Baptism represents death and burial of the old life and emergence to a new life in Jesus. By participating in this sacred ceremony, believers indicate their willingness for Jesus to begin a new life in them.

I like the inclusion of the word "walk" in this text. It implies that the postbaptismal life is a *process*, as opposed to a goal that's achieved the moment the candidate rises from the waters. It would be unrealistic to think the tendencies of the past could be wiped out in an instant. Rather, baptism is a new beginning—the turning of a corner. A placing of the hand in God's hand and saying, "Let's walk together from now on."

Jesus was baptized in the river Jordan when He was an adult. Matthew says that Jesus came from Galilee to the river and asked John to baptize Him, but John at first refused. He felt that Jesus should baptize him rather than the other way around. But Jesus answered: "Permit it to be so now, for thus it is fitting for us to fulfill all righteousness" (Matthew 3:15). Upon hearing this, John baptized his cousin. Can you imagine how he must have felt when the heavens opened and a voice said: "This is My beloved Son, in whom I am well pleased" (verse 17)? That was probably John's most memorable baptism!

It's important to note that Jesus wasn't baptized as a baby. We have biblical references of Jesus' boyhood, such as when He astounded the scholars in the Temple. Yet He waited until He was about 30 before He chose to be baptized. There are no biblical references to the baptism of babies. Since baptism is an outward symbol of a new birth and a *choice* made by the individual, the Bible teaches baptism only when an individual is old enough to repent of sin, accept Christ, and understand the truths of Scripture.

Another important aspect of Jesus' baptism is found in Mark 1:10: "And immediately, coming up from the water, He saw the heavens parting and the Spirit descending upon Him like a dove." Jesus was *in* the water. He was fully immersed during His baptism; He wasn't merely sprinkled.

And doesn't this make sense if the symbol of baptism is burial and resurrection—a death to an old way of life and an emergence to a new? Jesus' example reveals that biblical baptism comes through immersion.

When Paul was preaching in Damascus, he asked a question of those who'd gathered to listen. "And now why are you waiting? Arise and be baptized, and wash away your sins, calling on the name of the Lord" (Acts 22:16).

Baptism symbolizes the washing away of sins. It's an outward sign of belief. It's linked to salvation. It's the beginning of a new walk with Christ. It invokes the power of the Holy Spirit. Baptism is a beautiful, simple testimony of Christ's transforming grace and one's discovery of truth.

✦

In all my years of preaching, never have I found people with as strong a desire to know truth as that of the Muscovites! For the past three years I've conducted evangelistic meetings in Moscow at the Kremlin Congress Hall, the Olympic Stadium, and Plahanov University. Approximately 100,000 different people have attended the meetings, and we distributed 80,000 Bibles. Nearly 1 million Bible lessons were completed, and 4,000 persons were baptized. As a result, 12 new Adventist churches were established.

Hundreds lined up for hours before the meetings to be sure they secured a seat. During calls for baptism people ran down the aisles. After decades of Communism and banned Christianity nothing could hold them back when they heard the truth. One such man, Boris, is now a close friend.

Boris graduated from the highest ranking KGB academy. He trained to become a spy. His organizational ability put him in good stead as a potential leader for the Communist Party. A martial arts expert and top finisher in one of Russia's leading marathons, he was known in certain athletic circles in the former Soviet Union for his physical agility and speed. Then one day as he climbed his watchtower to stand guard at an important military installation, he slipped.

Lying in a hospital bed recovering from a broken back, Boris idled away the hours watching television. One chilly afternoon he watched in horror as the very KGB unit of which he was a part attacked civilians, putting down an uprising in the southern part of the U.S.S.R. He was sickened at the sight of the bloodshed of innocent civilians. For the first time Boris took the opportunity to think of his training with the KGB. He'd been taught to lie, cheat, steal, and commit murder. He'd become convinced that the end justified the means. But confined to that hospital bed, Boris had a chance to analyze where his life was headed, and he began to ask a lot of questions. What *is* the basis for moral values? How can I determine right and wrong? Is there life after death? Who is Jesus?

As these thoughts swirled in Boris's head, he longed for meaningful answers that he could stake his life on. Answers he could subject to the highest intellectual scrutiny. Answers that would last. And he asked himself another question: What do I know about God? The answer was simple: nothing. The KGB had taught him there was no God.

Somewhere Boris had heard somebody talk about a mountain sermon about loving your enemies that a man called Jesus had preached. He decided that he had to study that sermon, but where would he get it? He'd never held a Bible in his life.

The only religious institution he knew was the Russian Orthodox Church, so he wrote a letter to the bishop, requesting a copy of the mountain sermon preached by Jesus. As it so happens, the mailboxes of the Adventist pastor and the Russian Orthodox bishop were in close proximity to each other. Through God's providence the letter was wrongly directed, and wound up in the Adventist preacher's box instead.

The pastor visited Boris and read him the Sermon on the Mount. During the next several weeks of Boris's recovery the two men studied the Bible together, and Jesus' words penetrated his Communist upbringing. Boris asked Christ for purity of heart, meekness, gentleness of spirit, and the love detailed in the Beatitudes.

He read 2 Corinthians 5:17, which says: "Therefore, if anyone is in Christ, he is a new creation; old things have passed away; behold, all things have become new." And he asked Jesus for this newness of life, for the eradication of the guilt of his past sins. As Boris experienced peace and the fruits of conversion, his life took on new meaning.

Today Boris spends an hour in prayer and Bible study each morning before leaving his home to share the love of God with former Communists. He's a Christian pastor and studies the Bible with many others who wish to explore Christianity.

On the day I was to leave Moscow, Boris approached me with a gift. "Mark," this former KGB officer said to me, "I love you like a brother." He reached into his coat pocket and presented to me the gold-tipped fountain pen he'd used to write his final examinations in the KGB academy. He'd also used that same pen after his conversion to write sermons. Holding that symbolic gift in my hand, I could only marvel at Christ's transforming power.

Conversion is a change—a change of heart, a change of life, a change of attitudes. A change that only Christ can produce. And the life of Boris, along with thousands of others in the former Soviet Union, testifies to this life-giving, life-changing power of Jesus Christ.

✦

Don't you feel fortunate to live in a democratic country and have the freedoms we do? It isn't necessary to search for a Bible through the underground, as many Russians did for decades. You can simply jump into the car and head for the nearest bookstore. You can study and learn. Make choices. Make changes.

You're free to do these things, yet you too may be stymied by Western customs. Fear of change, the opinions of others, your scars from the past, the desire to get ahead materialistically—all these may dictate the course of your life, as it does many lives. If you let it, life can control you, rather than you controlling it.

Maybe it's time to stop as Boris did in his hospital room and ask, "What do I know about God? What would He have me to do?" Maybe it's time to stop, study, refocus, repent, and experience the new life Christ has promised. A new life that begins with the symbolic sacred ceremony of baptism. A life in process. A walk with God.

Caught by a Cult or Captured by the Truth?

When Steve, a freshman at the University of California at Berkeley, got involved in the "Ideal City Project," he had no inkling that he was joining a cult. However, soon after becoming a member of "The Family," he was spending 18 hours a day soliciting funds on the streets and getting only four hours of sleep a night. Then he discovered a life-changing secret in Revelation 14.

Sproul Plaza, at the center of the University of California at Berkeley campus, was crowded with tables that Monday afternoon. Various student groups displayed an assortment of books and brochures promoting everything from the Hillel Society to the Revolutionary Communist Youth Brigade.

Freshman Steve Kemperman was attracted to one large poster that read "Ideal City Project." It sounded like some kind of community endeavor, and Steve was interested in social work. The people at the table were very, very friendly, and he accepted an invitation to a free supper that evening at their communal home.

At the house, Steve was bombarded with flattering attention. He enjoyed an evening of good food and conversation. He'd never met so many enthusiastic, idealistic people at one time. They seemed dedicated to making the world a better place. Steve didn't know that this deliberate attempt to woo him was called "love bombing."

After that first positive night, Steve found himself going back again and again to find out more about this group that called themselves The Family. He listened to lectures, asked a lot of questions, but still couldn't quite figure out what made them tick. And yet he was being steadily drawn into their circle of love and idealism. In the end, Steve decided that the only way he could find out whether The Family had the truth or not was to join them for a while.

Steve discovered that The Family was actually something called The Holy Spirit Association for the Unification of World Christianity. This Unification Church followed a self-proclaimed messiah from Korea named Sun Myung Moon, who planned to usher in a new kingdom of world peace and promised to unite world Christianity into one kingdom. He proclaimed that objects from the fallen world, such as groceries, clothes, and gifts, must be purified with holy salt blessed by him.

Steve had many, many reservations about Moon's theology, but he was frequently told horror stories about what happened to those who left The Family. They invariably became empty, defeated shells of their former selves. Those who left were declared spiritually dead. Steve was taught to identify with Satan any doubts about Moon or thoughts about moving out of The Family. Negative thinking, as they called it, must be banished.

Along with other new followers in the cult, Steve was taught to express reservations about the Divine Leader with the rebuke "Come on, now, *no concepts.*" He was to give his mind over to the leaders and not think for himself. He was to look at everything and everyone outside the group as evil, part of Satan.

While their leader presided over a vast financial empire, Steve was soon spending 18 hours a day on the streets selling trinkets for The Family. Existing on four hours of sleep a night and completely subservient to the wishes of his superiors, he became a cog in a vast fund-raising machine. The church instructed him to solicit money under a number of different names. He told donors that their contributions were going to aid drug addicts or missionary work. "Satan deceived God's children," he was told, "so we're justified in deceiving Satan's children."

One night after a long day of fund-raising, he began to read the New Testament story of the prodigal son. Steve felt overwhelmed by the all-embracing, unconditional nature of God's love. That night his shouted chants turned into a quiet conversation with a God who seemed very near. He began to focus more on Jesus in his meditation. He felt touched by God. This experience was the beginning of Steve's eventual break with the Unification Church.

✦

How was Steve Kemperman caught by a cult? How did what appeared to be a loving group of people turn into such a trap? How can you avoid being sucked into a similar situation? The answer is that only by knowing the truth will you be able to detect a counterfeit.

Cults invariably center their truth on a charismatic leader. The guru, the prophet, the enlightened one, wields absolute authority in the group. He or she has all the answers. But absolute human authority creates an unhealthy dependence.

God respects human freedom. He's created us with the capacity of choice. Our relationship with Him is sacred and personal. No human being has the right to stand between us and God. No human being has the right to interfere with our moral choices. God has extended His grace to each individual through Jesus Christ, not through any other human being. The apostle Paul says that we're "justified freely by His grace through the redemption that is in Christ Jesus" (Romans 3:24). When churches or church leaders superimpose their demands on people, when they add to the gospel, when they establish their own conditions for

115

salvation, they aren't representing the God of the Bible.

Scripture encourages people to evaluate religious claims critically. "Beloved, do not believe every spirit, but test the spirits, whether they are of God; because many false prophets have gone out into the world" (1 John 4:1). You aren't to take the word of someone else or give away your own critical judgment, but rather you're instructed to evaluate truth for yourself. It would be impossible, of course, for you to investigate each church purporting to have truth today. More than 1,000 Christian denominations and groups operate in the United States alone! It would take a lifetime—maybe two or three—to investigate them all! But it *is* possible to compare each one with the unchanging biblical truth. The Bible is the only standard by which truth can be evaluated.

The Bible's last book, Revelation, reveals God's final message for humanity. It clearly outlines God's truth for today and provides a standard to evaluate churches claiming to have the truth. Let's examine some of Revelation 14.

"Then I saw another angel flying in the midst of heaven, having the everlasting gospel" (Revelation 14:6). God's true church preaches the gospel of Jesus Christ as its very foundation—Jesus as the Creator of the universe, Jesus as the only source of salvation, Jesus as our example, Jesus as the Son of God. This lies at the very core of God's final message. Christ is the center of every doctrine.

"But as many as received Him, to them He gave the right to become children of God, even to those who believe in His name" (John 1:12). Belief in His name. Belief in His saving grace. Belief that He's the divine Son of God. Belief in His salvation. Belief in His life-changing power. Belief in His Lordship. These are the fundamentals of Christianity.

The second half of verse 6 in Revelation 14 speaks about **"the everlasting gospel to [be preached] to those who dwell on the earth—to every nation, tribe, tongue,**

116

and people." God's final movement isn't some small isolated sect. It's a worldwide, international, mission-driven movement. This only makes sense. God wants to include all His beloved children in His last-day message. He wants all who desire it to spend eternity with Him in heaven. Therefore, He'll send His message around the world.

"Saying with a loud voice, 'Fear God and give glory to Him' " (Revelation 14:7). God's true church calls men and women to give glory to Him in their lifestyle. In everything they do, in every choice they make, in the way they design their daily lives, God's people remember the admonition found in 1 Corinthians 10:31: "Therefore, whether you eat or drink, or whatever you do, do all to the glory of God."

God's people choose to live a temperate, healthful lifestyle, knowing that to do so brings glory to God. The body is the temple of God, the crowning work of Creation. The Holy Spirit dwells within. The people of God want to do all in their power to take care of their bodies. In everything they eat, in everything they drink, in everything they do, they seek to bring honor and glory to His name.

"For the hour of His judgment has come" (Revelation 14:7). God's true church recognizes the signs foretold regarding the end-time and announces that these are the last days of earth's history. The hour of His judgment has come. History has run its course. The cosmic conflict between good and evil is soon to end. The monumental battle between Christ and Satan is almost finished. In heaven's halls of divine justice God reveals that He's done everything He can to save every human being. His love has relentlessly pursued each person. No one has an excuse for being lost. The entire universe will comprehend once and for all that God is both fully merciful and fully just. Before He comes, the destinies of every human being are settled forever in the judgment. (See Daniel 7:9, 10; Revelation 22:11, 12.)

"And worship Him who made heaven and earth, the sea and springs of water" (Revelation 14:7). One

117

of the great hallmarks of God's true church is God's final call to worship Him as Creator. Homage is due only to Him, not to any other person on the face of the earth. This is the basis of their worship—Christ as Creator. In an age of evolution in which some popular scientists deny His existence, His people give Him the deepest affections of their hearts and their supreme allegiance and tenderest affections.

How do we worship God as the Creator? What's the symbol of His creative power? The Bible Sabbath, of course! Written on the two tables etched in stone, the fourth commandment states: "For in six days the Lord made the heavens and the earth, the sea, and all that is in them, and rested the seventh day. Therefore the Lord blessed the Sabbath day and hallowed it" (Exodus 20:11).

God's true church will worship on the Sabbath, realizing that this is the day He has set aside as a commemoration of Creation week. We studied the Sabbath commandment just a few short chapters back. Remember the Bible text we discovered in Ezekiel? The Sabbath is a sign between us and God (Ezekiel 20:12). By observing this day that He has sanctified, we show that we recognize Him as our Lord.

God's true church leads men and women to faith in Jesus and obedience to His law. "Here is the patience of the saints; here are those who keep the commandments of God and the faith of Jesus" (Revelation 14:12).

A church is faithful to its Lord when it leads men and women to faithfulness to Christ and obedience to His commandments. Review the Ten Commandments for yourself. They're recorded in Exodus 20:2-17, along with the story of Moses' climbing Mount Sinai and receiving God's law on two tables of stone that God Himself had etched.

If a church teaches disrespect for parents, if a church advocates adultery, if a church teaches gods other than the one true God, if a church disregards the Sabbath, it cannot be the true church. All these precepts, and six more, are included in God's Ten Commandments. Use them when you evaluate a church.

I agree with Cal Thomas's opinion article that appeared in Michigan's *Herald-Palladium* on March 9, 1991. He said: "What moral impulse can a church exert when it conforms itself to the world rather than renewing its principles? Is it God who sets the agenda or, as the deists believed, did He just start the global ball rolling and then leave us to our own devices? . . . It is time for a revolution of the people who have not abandoned sound doctrine. Preachers and theologians who have departed from the truth must be asked to depart from their churches."

The true church does not conform itself to the world. The only safe course is strict adherence to the Bible. God set the agenda years ago. He hasn't changed it. It's up to His people to study His Word, to find out what He would have them to do, and to align themselves to those principles. Yes, it's a time to call Christians back to sound doctrine. However, we must first find a church that professes to teach sound doctrine, and then insist that it continue to do so.

Personally, I believe God has led me to such a church. Let me humbly share why. The Seventh-day Adventist Church believes that God is the final authority and that the individual's personal relationship with Him is paramount to any other relationship. It's the foundation upon which all other truth is built. Adventists openly acknowledge that Christ is the only head of the church. Salvation comes through Him and Him alone. We are saved by His grace alone. He is our Saviour and our Lord. We love Him enough to obey Him. We believe His Word enough to follow it. We are convinced that His way is wiser than our own.

The Seventh-day Adventist Church believes in clean living and a healthful lifestyle. We abstain from tobacco and drinking alcohol, and we advocate a healthful diet.

The Seventh-day Adventist Church is a Bible-based denomination. We believe the only document recorded as having come directly from God's hand, the Ten Commandments, is the basis for all morality. His law doesn't restrict our happiness. It provides the foundation for happiness. The Sabbath command in the heart of God's law calls us to worship Him as our Creator, thereby finding our true rest in Him.

The Seventh-day Adventist Church believes that we're living in the last days of earth's history. Time is short. Jesus' second coming provides hope for a world in deep trouble. In countries that have been closed to Christians for years, God has opened up the opportunities for witness so that all may choose to follow Him.

The Seventh-day Adventist Church is a thriving and growing international denomination. We currently have churches in 204 of the 233 countries or areas of the world. Twenty of those countries were entered for the first time during the past four years.

✦

Travel with me for a few moments around the world and witness God's incredible power. More than 12,000 people streamed into the Kremlin Congress Hall in Moscow night after night to hear God's Word. The Kremlin was the citadel of Communism, the center of atheistic propaganda. Or come with me to Moscow's Olympic Stadium, where more than 50,000 different people attended our Bible presentations. I've personally seen the eagerness in the eyes of tens of thousands of sincere truth seekers in Poland, Hungary, Yugoslavia, and the countries of Eastern Europe.

More than 10 million people a week watch It Is Written's television program in Brazil, and millions more view it around the world. Recently the Voice of Prophecy's radio program enrolled 1 million new students in Brazil. It too is heard around the world. God's message is spreading like wildfire!

In January of 1994 Adventist World Radio began a powerful broadcast from two 250-kilowatt transmitters in the new republic of Slovakia. The station began regular 24-hour broadcasts of Christian programming in Arabic, Czech, English, French, German, and in India's four major languages. That means we're now covering all central and eastern Africa, all India, and all the Middle East with the good news of Jesus Christ.

And then there's the newly built Adventist Media Center in Tula, Russia. Gospel radio programs are sent out from there in eight languages every day. These programs, which are involving 65,000 people in Bible study, cover southern Europe and much of Asia, including parts of China. The broadcasts are transmitted through five of the Russian government's most powerful facilities. Transmitters, which used to jam radio signals coming from the West, are now used to proclaim the gospel of Jesus Christ. Adventist World Radio carries the radio version of the It is Written program. It now covers three quarters of the world's population!

Yes, the good news is going out to the billions. From one end of the globe to the other, God is opening doors and the word is going forward. Every Sabbath nearly 8 million Seventh-day Adventists meet in 36,000 churches around the world, reading the same Bible promises, worshiping the same God, all looking forward to Jesus' soon coming.

But at this moment I'm not interested in the vast overall picture. I'm interested only in you. I know that Jesus knows you by name, that He cares about what happens to you, and that He wants you to spend eternity in heaven with Him.

Will you open your heart to Jesus right now? Will you say, "Jesus, I accept You both as my Saviour and Lord"? Will

121

you determine, "Lord, wherever You lead me, I will follow"? Why not tell Him right now that you're His child and that you have one desire—to do whatever He asks?

For your personal series of free Bible study guides or for more information regarding Seventh-day Adventists
Phone 1-800-253-3000

Experience happiness no problem can take away!

When problems weigh you down, where do you turn? Millions of people have found the answer in a relationship with Jesus Christ.

Happiness Digest shows how you too can experience His joy and guidance, and offers help in the calm assurance that God is in ultimate control and very much interested in your life.